Keep on Laughing

John A. Walton

A Father's Prayer

Build me a son, O Lord, who will be strong enough to know when he is weak, and brave enough to face himself when he is afraid; one who will be proud and unbending in honest defeat and humble and gentle in victory.

Build me a son whose wishbone will not be where his backbone should be; a son who will know Thee and that to know himself is the foundation stone of knowledge.

Lead him, I pray, not in the path of ease and comfort, but under the stress and spur of difficulties and challenge. Here let him learn to stand up in the storm; here let him learn compassion for those who fail.

Build me a son whose heart will be clear, whose goal will be high, a son who will master himself before he seeks to master other men; one who will learn to laugh, yet never forget to weep; one who will reach into the future, yet never forget the past.

And after all these are his, add, I pray, enough of a sense of humor, so that he may always be serious, yet never take himself to seriously. Give him humility, so that he may always remember the simplicity of true greatness, the open mind of true wisdom, the meekness of true strength.

Then I, his father, will dare to whisper, "I have not lived in vain."
(Douglas MacArthur)

Phil. 1-6

Printed by:
A&J Printing
P.O. Box 518
Nixa, MO 65714

Published by: J.A.W.'S Publishing

Order From:
Sgt. John A. Walker
530 Alger Ave.
Manistique, MI 49854
Phone: 906-341-2082
E-mail: jawspub@juno.com

Library of Congress Cataloging-In-Publication Data
Walker, John A.

3rd Printing

ISBN 0-9639798-2-5

Sgt. John A. Walker writes for:
Manistique Pioneer Tribune
212 Walnut St.
Manistique, MI 49854
Phone: 906-341-5200

These stories are written to show the humorous side of working as a Game Warden- living in Michigan U.P. They are not meant to offend anyone and are just the writer's version of the stories as he heard or saw them happen. No names are used in the stories without prior approval.

INDEX

The picture on the cover of this book is the man talked about in the story titled, O! Not Again. This is the "BIG" Northern Pike he caught up here on Big Bay De Noc that last summer.

Gordon was from down in Dori, MO, near where my wife and family lived. As I state in the story, he was one of the finest Christian men I ever had the pleasure of meeting. He always seemed to have the same type grin you see in the photo of him with his prize fish.

The fish was 46" long and weight almost thirty pounds. What a catch!

I ask his wife in church one Sunday if she happened to have a picture of her husband with his prize fish? She opened her Bible and took out the photo I used to have the cover printed. I guess this more than anything tells the feelings of this couple that I tried to get across in my tale. Fishing together was just a way of life for them.

Forewarned

Conservation Officer's Stories
Upper Michigan Tales from a Game Warden's Perspective

From The Land Where Big Fish Live

Well, when a person tries to think through some things there are bound to be changes before he even gets started.

I was going to call my next book *"Having a Super (Yooper) Bad Day"*, but before I even got started I was talking to some bookstore people about my third book. When I told them I was hung up between the above title or *"From The Land Where Big Fish Live"* and they all voted for the *"Big Fish"* title. So, change number one took place even before I got started.

It seems that the one comment I received over and over from my first two books *(A Deer Gets Revenge & A Bucket of Bones)* was that people wanted more fishing and trapping stories. So, I added some to this book.

This is the third book in my series that is made up of stories from my newspaper column in the Manistique Pioneer Tribune. I have been writing a weekly article for this local paper for a number of years now. In the fall of 1993, I came out with my first book called *A Deer Gets Revenge*. In the first year I had 13,000 copies of this book self-published. It was unreal.

In 1994 my second book called *A Bucket of Bones* came out and I had 8,000 of these printed up. Between the two books, in the first year, I had 21,000 books self-published.

I started these book projects because I wanted to have a scholarship fund at the little church I attend to help the youth from the church go to college. I promised myself that $1.00 from each book I sold would go into this scholarship fund. In the first year we had over $10,000 in the fund and had given out seven scholarships to college students.

There is good clean humor in all my stories and all the stories are true. They may be told with a "backwoods" flavor, but they are all true stories. Everybody has their favorite Game Warden story, but the Game Warden has a few favorites of his own, too.

There are a few serious stories in the books about growing up and living in the U.P. (Upper Michigan). I guess when you had the great parents I had you just want to let people know about it. So, each book has a story or two about Mom and Dad.

I have received letters from people all over the country that came across my first two books. Everybody from college presidents, corporation presidents, housewives, and school kids that just love the books. It seems that in this day and age when everything is so wound up, we all like to sit down once in a while and read something that will not tax our brain to hard. My books seem to fit the bill.

This book covers everything from fishing, bow hunting, trapping, regular hunting, and flat messing up, to just living in the backwoods. It is meant to just get one's mind back to thinking about nothing and giving the mind a rest.

This book has a number of pages of colored pictures taken when hunting during the fall here in the U.P. There are also some old pictures from days gone by. It also has some pictures to back up the title of the book, *From The Land Where the Big Fish Live.*

People ask me all the time where all the stories come from? I tell them when you work in a district that touches three of the five Great Lakes, (Michigan, Superior, and Huron) then you have 340 inland lakes, covering more than 20,861 acres in the county you live in alone, plus 734 miles of rivers and streams, you are bound to have some crazy things happen! Add to this a bunch of young guys out there playing cowboys and Indians in the dark and anything can happen.

After my first two books came out, I started getting letters from people from all over the country that wanted to tell me their favorite Game Warden or outdoor story. Everybody has a favorite.

The stories in my third book will be told with the same good clean humor that all my stories are told with. For two very good reasons: Number 1, I could not sleep nights if I used the kind of language that is to common in so many things we read and hear in this day and age. Number two: (and maybe the most important) my little hillbilly wife would whip me in my sleep if she ever found out that I used the wrong type of language in any of the stories in my books. It just gets too hard to explain to all the guys at coffee how a two hundred and thirty pound guy got whipped by his little wife. So, this book continues with the good clean family-style humor that was found in my first two books.

Remember as you read this book, all the stories are true and happened to real people. They could also happen to you anywhere you may live. I have people from all over the country write me and tell me that they know someone in their town that had the same type adventure as the person in my story.

So happy reading…

Dear Friends,

Since my first book titled *A Deer Gets Revenge* was published we have been able, with the Lord's help, to self-publish over 50,000 copies of my six books.

When you think that the reason I wrote my first book was hopefully to make enough to start a scholarship fund at Bethel Baptist Church here in Manistique, it has been a totally amazing trip. For someone that had no idea how to write a book, let alone self-publish it and then sell it, someone has to be helping him out. In fact I still have no idea how you are really suppose to do things, I just figure if something is working why change it, just try to improve it.

I have shipped books all over the country and to at least a dozen other countries. People seem to just like the way the stories are told and the good, clean humor that is in the books.

With this fall (2001) we will go over the $40,000 mark raised for the scholarship fund. When the scholarships checks are sent to the students this fall semester we will have given out more than $20,000 in college scholarships. It is sure hard to believe.

I am still doing the weekly *Fish Report* for the Manistique Pioneer Tribune. It just seems there is no end to the great stories you hear and all the things people like to read about. The *Fish Report* has not changed in over twenty years; it still usually talks about everything except fishing. Honestly I do make mention of fishing once in a great while.

I would just like to say **"Thank You"** to all you out there that have purchased one of my books and made my dream of a scholarship come true. But I have to wonder why you did not order the whole set? You see if you order them early enough you can read them before Christmas, then give them away for Christmas gifts. Just remember not to bend the covers back.

Thanks again for all your help,
                                            JOHN

Chapter 1

Conservation Officer's Stories
Upper Michigan Tales from a Game Warden's Perspective

Backwoods Ladies

I learned quick and sure that there is a whole different way of doing things in the Great North Woods. There was more than one time that the lady of the house set me straight about the who and why of things. These are a couple of those stories.

Ladies of the Woods

Up where I worked, for years, trapping was a way of life. In the past number of years it was done more for the sport of it than because of what money could be made doing it. Trapping is important up here with all the lakes and streams in the area. If the crops of beaver and other fur-bearing animals are not harvested and managed they tend to take over an area. Forests are ruined, roads are wrecked, bridges for trains can be undermined, and while farm fields and drains are ruined. Those families that have just been at it for years do most of the trapping. This is how things were done back in the "good old days" in the U.P.

A number of years back it was required that all beaver and otter be tagged before they could be sold. In fact, back when I was a kid, one of the biggest events of the year was held at the local Ontonagon Fire Hall. On this day, all the trappers would bring all their hides down to the Fire Hall. The local Game Warden would be there to check the hides over and tag them with a State seal so they could be sold.

After this was done, there would be a number of fur buyers walking around making bids for the stacks of hides to the trappers that had taken them. This fur buyer would walk up and check out your hides to see what kind of job you had done stretching them. He would also check to see what grade the fur was. As he did this I can remember he always had money, 100s, 20s and 10s between his fingers. As he talked with the trapper about his hides,

1

he would all this time be waving his fist full of money up and down in front of his face, then he would make his bid for the furs.

Later, as the years went by the trappers came by the Conservation Department Field Stations to get their furs tagged. Once in a while, there would be a family of trappers that had so many hides that they would ask me to swing by their place, look the hides over, and tag them there. This is what I did on this one particular day.

I got to this new house overlooking Indian Lake. This family had trapped for years together. They always took a lot of mink, otter, and some beaver. Their hides were always first class and well taken care of. I would go out there and meet someone from the family, and we would go out into the garage to look the hides over.

On this day when I got to their house, I found that only the lady of the house was at home. I asked if I could look the hides over, and she said she would show them to me. We went out into the garage and as usual there were a number of prime, well taken care of hides. I looked them over and tagged those that needed tagging. We were then standing there talking when I mentioned what a good job her husband and boys did skinning out and taking care of their pelts. From the look on her face, I knew right away I had said something wrong.

She stood there and looked at me for a minute then stated, "I'll have you know that I do most of the skinning and take care of the hides after the men catch them." What could I say! Here was this nice, pleasant lady, well taken care of and living in a nice neat new house. It never dawned on me that she would be skinning and fleshing out fur-bearing animals! Boy, did I have a lot to learn.

I was to find out that in several trapping families it is true that the women take care of the skinning, fleshing, and stretching of the hides after the men bring them in.

Ladies, Too

Back when I was a kid, and even after I started to work as a Game Warden, the officers sold all the beaver licenses from their homes. There was one interesting twist to a beaver license. They had to be purchased before the start of the season and back then you could only get five beaver on a license.

It seemed when the law worked this way there were a number of women that took up trapping. They had to if the husband wanted to get more then five beaver. If he wanted a few more, the kids got a license and took up trapping. Then even Grandma and Grandpa. It was just the way it worked.

I can remember asking my dad one time how come this one family always had so many beaver licenses, therefore so many beaver. I can remember my dad saying, "It's easy the way they do it, son. They buy a license for all the kids and half the cows, and then they catch the five beaver pelts for each license."

When A Lie is Not a Lie

One time there were a number of arrests made for taking otter illegally. I had to attend a pre-trial hearing up in Federal Court in Marquette. It seems that when a group of trappers had come in and tagged their otter they had lied about just where they had caught them. The Federal Agents were trying to make a big case out of this.

I had always been taught from my youth to tell the truth and let the cards fall where they may. When I was asked by the Federal Prosecutor if it was true that these trappers lied on their tagging slips I stated, "Yes sir, they all do. "The Federal Officers were upset and the Prosecutor was dumbfounded. You see, back then if what the people were doing on a minor violation was a local practice, they would not be prosecuted for it. Instead they were warned that what they were doing was illegal.

The prosecutor asked me what I meant. I knew this Federal Prosecutor had once been a local Prosecutor over in Houghton in the Copper Country. I also knew he was an avid brooktrout fisherman. So, I said, "If you go out and catch a real nice mess of nice large brooktrout from your secret spot what do you tell those that asked you where you caught them? You don't really lie to those that asked you where you caught your brooktrout, you just send them off in the wrong direction to try and catch their own." I said, "These trappers are no different than a good brooktrout fisherman trying to protect his secret fishing hole. We know they

3

are not telling us right where they caught the otter, but somewhere in the area." He looked at me with a smile on his face that said he understood. It is just one of those times when the truth is just not really the truth, but kind of close.

Silent Screams

If you are a lady and want to live an abnormal life just marry a Game Warden with the hours he comes and goes, projects he works on, and the things he drags home.

It was nothing for my wife to open the top of the frig after I had spent a night working illegal fish spearers to find a half dozen Northern Pike staring at her. There was always something in the freezer or frig being kept for evidence or that had been turned over to the local Game Warden, because it was illegal for someone to have it.

One day a local trapper came by and gave me a couple of Pine Martin pelts that he had. This trapper had caught these Pine Martins in his mink sets and, at the time, it was illegal for a trapper to be in possession of them. We talked for a while, then I took the pelts from the Pine Martins down and threw them in the corner of our freezer in the basement.

Now, our freezer sits over against the sidewall of our basement in an area where there is not much light. Usually, when you go down to the freezer, you have to dig around till you find what you are looking for, then hold it up to the light to make sure it is what you want.

One day, my wife was trying to figure out what to have for supper. She went down to the freezer to get some meat. She turned on the basement lights and went over to look for a package of meat. On the dark side of the basement, she opens the freezer lid and reaches in to feel for packages of meat. When she moves a few packages around, all of a sudden she is holding a handful of cold, damp, fleshy Pine Martin!!

My wife jumps back and screams for all she is worth. (I asked her later what good that did seeing she was home by herself and nobody could hear the scream anyway.) She then went and got a flashlight to see what in the world she had grabbed hold of. It was just one of the many surprises a Game Warden's wives might come across from his adventures. I have often wondered what we ended up having for supper that night.

By the way, if you come to my house now you will see a light mounted over our freezer, and you can turn it on and see what is in the freezer before you put your hand in it and start feeling around.

We Blew It!

On this night during the firearm deer season, we were out working shiners. We had patrolled north of Gulliver and swung around to hit the Green School road going into the Port Inland property.

After leaving US-2 there were a number of houses for a ways, then the houses stopped and you came to some big fields before one of the Inland Quarries. There were always a lot of deer in this area, but it was hard to get them near the road to shoot while shining.

My partner and I headed down the Green School road and shut off our headlights as we cleared the last of the houses. We then ran to the edge of the woods into the area of the fields without using any lights at all. As we neared the fields, we saw a car turn on its headlights and shine off to the passenger side of the road.

Since we wanted to get where we could see what they were doing, we cut down a 2-track on my side of the road, across the field and back on another 2-track, so that we were right behind them on the blacktop again. We sat and watched them shine the field for a minute then turned on the spotlights and blue light to check them out for firearms. (They could shine at this time, but then could not have a firearm with them.)

I went up to the driver's side as my partner went up to the passenger side of the vehicle. To our surprise, in this car that had been sitting along side the road in the dark without any headlights on, just shining a spotlight across the field, sat three women. There was not a man to be found. About the same time we noticed the three women, we saw an empty gun case on the floor in the front near the front seat.

Oh, crud!!! We blew it!! We were sure the men had to be out in the field with the firearm!

We asked the women to step out of the car, so we could ask them some questions with little chance of them telling us who was out in the field with the gun from the empty gun case. As they got out of the car and moved to the back, I shined my flashlight down on the front floor, and-to my surprise-saw a lever action rifle on the floor!

I picked it up, and it was loaded. I took the rifle, unloaded it, and carried the spotlight back to the patrol unit to ask the women what they were up to.

One answered and said, "Our husbands told us to stay away from the bars with all the hunters in the area, so we decided to go shining for deer. We bought the spotlight at Holiday and came out this way looking for deer." What could I say?

I went back to the patrol unit to make out some tickets. As I was doing this, I picked up the spotlight that the three women had purchased at Holiday a couple of hours before and on the back it read, "Warning! In most states even if it is legal to shine for deer, it is illegal to do it when in possession of a firearm!"

I guess those warning labels just do not always work.

Chapter 2

Conservation Officer's Stories
Upper Michigan Tales from a Game Warden's Perspective

Hot Lips Returns

Well, I guess everyone knows who the most famous star of my first book was. It seems like everyone liked the story about Hot-lips. I had college kids from down south that read the stories say, "They can't be true, those things could not happen to anyone." But, they do. Every story in each of my books is true. What makes them sound like they could not have happened is the way they are told, added to, then re-told.

There is only one person that I know who could have all the things happen to him that this guy had happen to him and still be alive to tell people about it. I have to wonder about all the stories. I know his brother gets deer, I know his dad gets deer, but does this guy ever get one?

O' My Aching Head

The star of my book *"A Deer Gets Revenge"* was out on another hunting trip. (I have to say one word of warning. If you know where Hot Lips is hunting, you may want to find a different area of the woods to hunt in.) It was firearm deer season and a nice warm fall day. Our hunter had not seen anything from his blind, so he decided to walk around and look for deer sign.

He had spent some time walking down a runway and found a spot where there were a lot of deer signs. He had been walking for quite a while and was warm with all his hunting gear on, so he decided to sit down under a big pine tree to rest. From where he was sitting he could look over a deer runway and just maybe something would come along.

Our mighty hunter must have fallen asleep. All of a sudden, our hunter realized he must have dozed off and just woke up! But, as he went to jump up and make sure nothing was moving on the runway he realized he had a terrific headache. He slumped down, put his hand up to the top of his head, and felt something wet and sticky!

As he pulled his hand away and saw he was bleeding, he realized that the blood covered the top of his head! The first thought that went through his mind was that he had been accidentally shot while sitting there resting under this large pine tree. All he could think of was, "I've been shot by some other hunter!" as a cold sweat covered his body. He felt his head again trying to figure out how badly he was hurt while wondering what to do. (You know what they always say in those old western movies, "The one that gets you, you will never hear being fired.") He had not heard a thing.

As he sat there in a cold sweat, he looked around trying to figure out what had happened and saw, lying right next to him on the ground, a large, dead branch out of the big pine tree he was sitting under! Now, you have to remember, he knew the branch was not there when he sat down, and he had not placed his hat under the branch.

So, our hunter got looking around and finally figured things out. Out of all the millions of trees in the woods, he had picked one to rest under that just at the right time was going to shed one of its rather large branches for the winter right on his head as he slept.

At least, what happened this time was not his fault? Maybe hunter's orange hard hats for deer season?

Watch for Those Whooshes!

There was another time old Hot-lips was out making plans for getting the "Big" one. This time he was setting up for some bow hunting. He had picked a perfect spot and looked the area over for a place to put his bait pile.

He then looked around for a perfect place to set his tree stand up. Now, you have to remember that up here in the U.P. the deer are really smart. We have deer running around in the woods with bad necks from having to keep looking up in the trees for bow hunters up there waiting in them. It is just not normal for deer to spend all fall walking around checking trees.

Our hunter found the perfect tree, climbed up and placed his bow stand where he wanted it-just "so high" off the ground. (This is important, because you don't want to have too far to fall if you fall asleep in your tree stand. Could this ever happen to our accident-prone hunter?)

After he got his stand fastened to the tree and got things ready, he climbed up onto the stand to see how the view was to his bait pile. PERFECT!! Except for that one branch that was hanging right out in front of him just enough to obstruct his perfect shot at any deer standing on the runway. He would fix that.

He tried to reach it from the tree stand and could not. He climbed around trying to get hold of it but could not, so he climbed down to the ground. Here he came up with a much better idea. Seeing the branch was too high and too far out to reach by hand, he would fix it.

He tied a rope around the head of his trusty hatchet he always carried. Our hunter stepped back and threw the hatchet up, so that it wound around the branch a number of times and tightened up. It had twisted around the branch just like he knew it would. (He had watched Knights of the Round Table do this same thing and pull themselves up over the castle walls, so he was all set.)

He got ready, stepped back till the rope was tight, then pulled on the rope for all he was worth in order to pull this dead branch that was in his way off of the tree!

WHOOSH!!

As the axe unwound from around the branch, it went sailing right by his head before he could even figure out what had happened or what to do!! He checked to make sure he still had both ears and all his hair, then figured just maybe he had better try alternate plan three! It just might be safer.

Only to Me

It could only happen to one of this crowd. It seems that this party had a bow stand set up in a beautiful area. There were a lot of deer signs, some nice big scrapes, and a number of nice rubs from a big buck.

Our hunter spent day after day sitting there waiting for the "Big" one to walk by. The scrapes were being worked and there were signs all over to show that the big buck was still around. He spent all season waiting on this buck, seeing some does and fawns, but never getting a good look at the big buck. Right up to the end of the season he stuck it out.

As next bow season rolled around, he went out to scout the area over. Sure enough, there were still signs, so he walked over to where his bait pile had been.

There sitting right on top of where his bait pile had been was the perfect shed from a fourteen-point buck! Both sides. As if the "Big" buck wanted to kind of rub it in as to who had won out last season.

I know it's true, because he showed me the antlers when he told me this story. You can bet he is going to live out there this fall. The only thing is, with his luck, a car hit his monster buck during the summer.

Chapter 3

Conservation Officer's Stories
Upper Michigan Tales from a Game Warden's Perspective

A True Game Warden

Well, all red-blooded American boys need to have a dog or two around just to have someone to listen to them. I guess we always had a dog when I was growing up. If things got too bad with all the girls around, I would go out and crawl into the doghouse with my dad's dogs. He had two Springer's, Jack and Peg, who had a doghouse big enough for both of them and a couple of kids. Many a happy time was spent in there talking to and playing with the dogs.

Even now, I have my hunting dog, Rocky, that for some reason my teenage daughter thinks is hers. Rocky sleeps in her room, sleeps at her feet as she watches TV, and goes nuts whenever she pulls into the yard. Rocky is a Golden Retriever that someone gave to us. A party that professionally trains hunting dogs trained him, and he is one in a million.

This story is about man's best friend.

Who Can You Trust, If Not Your dog?

Over in an area near Big Manistique Lake there is a little town called Curtis. These lakes in this area are famous for their walleye fishing, day and night. In fact, the local people around the area have worked with the state Department of Natural Resources for years on a walleye-rearing project.

In these lakes when the walleye spawn in the spring of the year, they come up in the early evening to real shallow water right along the edge of the lake. You can spot them with a spotlight or flashlight when they are spawning in this shallow water, because walleye have a real red eye that glows in the dark when hit with a light.

On this evening, there was a party that had a plan to take a few of these walleye when they came in to spawn. Now, as I stated, walleye come in to spawn right after dark, spend a couple of hours, and move back out into the deeper water of the lake. This party had a plan. He was going to run a gill net out from shore into the lake a little ways into the path of the spawning walleye.

(You put the net right from shore out into the lake in an area you can wade to. The walleye move along the shore to their spawning area and are caught in the gill net.)

Our party took his net and went just down the beach a little ways from his cottage and placed the net in the location where he knew the walleye would be. He then returned home and went into the cottage. He set his alarm and made plans to get up in a couple of hours to go down and pull his net and get his catch of illegal walleye. All was going great.

The net was set after dark when the walleye should be running, and he dozed off waiting for his alarm to go off. Sure enough, off went the alarm just as he had planned. He shut the alarm off and rolled over. The next thing he knew there was light coming in through the windows and it was early daylight. He had fallen back to sleep, and his net was still set out in the lake!

Since there was no longer any chance of sneaking back out under cover of darkness to retrieve his gill net, he came up with his next best plan. It seems that our party owned a little dog that barked at anyone and anything that was around. So, our netter took his trusty little dog to be his watchdog, and headed down to the beach to pull his gill net.

All went great. He got to the area where his net was at first light with his "watchdog". He looked around and saw nobody. Since his "watchdog" dog was not making a fuss, the coast was clear! Our fisherman moved out to the water, started to pull his gill net in, and sure enough, there were a few walleye in it. After he got the net into shore, he wound up his net and catch.

All of a sudden, he realized that his little "watchdog" was not running around him anymore and also was not making a sound. This was not good! He slowly looked around and, at first, did not see a thing. Then, he looked over in an area where there were some steps that came down the bank to the beach. As he looked under the steps into the shaded area, he saw his dog, his dog that was now licking his chops, after just having eaten a sandwich, and having enjoyed it. A sandwich being held and fed to his "watchdog" by the local Game Warden. Who now had that look on his face that told him that he had been had.

I heard parts of this story from both sides, so you have to weigh it for the truth.

A Perfect Count

This local Game Warden had worked this same area in the U.P. for years. This officer had a way about him that everyone knew, and he had about the dumbest luck in catching people any of us ever saw. He was really a hard worker, but not all the time was his skill alone what helped him to catch violators.

On this day, our local Game Warden was working an area where he knew there were a lot of steelhead trout spawning. He walked the stream till he came to an area that had a big pool where there were some nice trout spawning. In this area, there was no place to hide close to the stream. A high bank overlooked the pool where the trout were. As the violators would come up to the stream, they could check along the bank and make sure nobody was in the area.

So, our Game Warden friend had to come up with a plan of attack. He moved back into the woods away from the stream till he found an old hollow tree that he could hide in. But, he had to get to the stream without using a light when he heard the violators in the water after the trout. He thought about it and figured he had it worked out. He got in the area of his hiding tree and paced it off to the high bank overlooking the pool with the trout in it. He then paced it off back to the tree again. The officer did this a number of times till he had it all worked out to just so many steps from his hiding place to the bank where he would shine his light down on the outlaws and have them! Good, the officer would be back after dark.

After dark, our Game Warden returned and checked for bait. Sure enough, the trout are still lying in the pool. He paces it off to his tree and sits down to wait for action. Maybe tonight.

After a couple of hours, he heard someone coming through the woods down to the area of the high bank. Down over the bank into the stream they go. He gives them time to get into action, than stands up to pace it off and make his move. He starts out pacing and counting. One, two...ten, eleven....seventeen, eighteen....all is going great... just a few more paces.... twenty-five...AAAAAAAHH!! Goes our Game Warden over the bank into the stream of spawning trout (now being speared trout) amongst the perpetrators!

Splash!! Here lands our Game Warden right in their lap! But, believe it or not, as this officer's luck would have it, they were so surprised at seeing this flying Game Warden that they all just stood there while he lifted himself up out of the water and arrested them.

Chapter 4

Conservation Officer's Stories
Upper Michigan Tales from a Game Warden's Perspective

Fish Stories

Well, I guess everyone has their favorite "Fish Story" they like to tell. When you work as a Game Warden, you get a chance to see a few and hear a lot more. The following stories are some that I came across in my travels. You have to be a true "Yooper" (a person that lives in Michigan's Upper Peninsula) to understand these stories and how we love our hunting and fishing. The following was given to me at church one Sunday. It is not new, just to us "Yoopers".

Yooper Creation Story

In da Beginning dere was nuttin!

Den on da first day God created da U.P.

On da second day He created da partridge, da deer, da bear, da fish, and da ducks and geese.

On da third day He said, "Let there be "Yoopers"~to roam da U.P.

On da fourth day He created da udder world down below, an on da fifth day....

He Said, "Let there be TROLLS to live in da world down below.

On da sixth day He created, "Da Big Mac Bridge" so da TROLLS would have a way to get to heaven.

God saw it was good and on the seventh day He rested and went fishing.

O! Not Again!

One great thing about being a Conservation Officer is all the nice people you get to meet. In the area of Big Bay De Noc there was this couple that came up from Missouri to spend the summers. They had been coming up to God's Country for years to "The Land Where the BIG Fish Live", and once you met this man and his wife, you would never forget him. When he came up to say, "Hi!" and shake your hand, you soon realized something about him. Now, I have a good-sized hand, but it would get lost in his. Then, that big hillbilly grin would just make your day. He had been a successful businessman and rancher down near Dora, MO, but he had a summer place up near Bay De Noc. Man, did he like to fish!

Now, down in Missouri you have to remember they catch a few pan fish, a bass or two, maybe some catfish, but nothing like we have up here in the land where the BIG fish live. So each summer day he could he would spend his time out on Bay De Noc with his wife after real fish.

One day, he was out there enjoying the great summer weather and just being able to be out on the bay. All of a sudden, he had a strike!! He knew right away it was a monster, bigger then any fish he had ever caught, by the way his line played out. He relaxed to work the monster fish a while and tire it out, so he could get it up next to the boat. Like I said, this was a big fish, and it took some time. But, it was going to be worth the wait.

After he got a glance at it a couple of times as it came near the surface, he knew it was the biggest fish he had ever hooked. Finally, his monster fish got tired out, and he worked it over next to the boat. Then his problems really began!

Now, like I said, on this day he had his wife with him. Our fisherman was holding his line tight to keep his monster fish from flipping loose and "ALL" his wife had to do was net this monster, right? The only problem was they had not planned on ever catching a fish this size, seeing they were from out of the area. All they had was a landing net they used for their average Ozark-size fish. After a few times of trying to net this big fish, the wife finally.... managed to knock the hook out of the fish's mouth with the net while trying to get it into the net and off swam our monster sized fish.

I often asked him if he ever took his wife back out fishing with him again? He would just give you that big hillbilly grin of his. I had a large landing net that was used for salmon fishing at my house that I gave to him-just in case.

Well, a couple of summers ago he was back out on Big Bay De Noc and hooked another one of those dream fish. This one he managed to play around, get up next to the boat, and even land. It was a nice big Northern Pike, a once in a lifetime size. He got it back to the trailer and knew he wanted to get this one mounted because chances were that never again would a person ever hook one this big. But, our fisherman had no place at his trailer to freeze his trophy, because it was so big. Off he went to a friend's house to place it in their freezer. When he got to this friend's farmhouse, there was nobody at home. So, this being the U.P., he just went in the house, down to the basement, and placed it in their freezer and left.

When the lady of the house returned home for supper, she found this monster Northern Pike in her freezer, and she figured she would have some fun. After supper, she called our fisherman at his trailer, got him on the phone, and said, " Thanks for the fish you dropped off! It tasted great, but it was just too big for my husband and I to eat in one meal."

Needless to say there was dead silence on the other end of the phone, till she could not hold it any longer and started laughing. Then, our fisherman knew it was all a joke.

None of us ever thought when we all were teasing him about finally catching a "BIG" fish that it would be his last summer with us up in God's country. Now that hillbilly handshake and grin are gone, but I guess God just wanted him to catch that one dream fish from "The Land Where the BIG Fish Live" before He took him home.

Trolling

There is nothing a true "Yooper" likes to do better than to pull a good one over on an innocent "troll" that just moved north from below the bridge.

It seems that there was this party that worked for the government and transferred north from down in "Troll" Land. I guess he just wanted to get a little taste of heaven, so he packed his bags and moved to the U.P. This did not make him a "Yooper", but it did make him fair game.

When the warm weather of spring came around, some of Eino and Teivo's cousins told our transplanted "Troll" they would like him to go fishing with them. Great!! This is just what he moved up to the U.P. for. He was not really a fisherman, in fact had never done any of it, but was willing to learn.

Plans were made to go smelt fishing, a first for our transplant (make sure you read in the glossary what a smelt is, so you can keep up with this story). He was told by his two new fishing partners (Eino and Teivo's cousins) that you smelt fish at night (well, everybody knows that-even a "Troll"), so he should bring a lantern and a five gallon bucket, When the smelt are really biting it is nothing to fill a 5-gallon bucket full of them! They told him what other equipment to bring, and they picked him up that evening after dark and off they went.

Since our two "Yooper" natives had their secret smelting spot, they got there with no problem. Because they wanted their new fishing buddy to have the best spot, they helped him out with his lantern, 5-gallon smelting bucket, and his fishing equipment. They got their "Troll" all set up, explained to him how you went about smelting, and set off to another hole upstream so they would not mess each other up. Off the two went as our new-lander got his gear all ready and went to smelting.

In just no time at all Eino and Teivo's cousins were back to his smelting spot!! With both their 5-gallon buckets full of flopping smelt!! They asked how he was doing? With a shocked look on his face, seeing their 10-gallons of smelt, he told them, "None yet." The smelt were there. He could see them, but he had not caught a single one yet. Our "Yoopers" told our fast-learning "Troll" that they had plenty for all of them with their two 5-gallon buckets full, so they would just head back home and share what they had caught with him. It sounded fair enough to him. He picked up his gear and off they went.

It was some time later that our transplant was telling another "Yooper" about his first smelting trip. How he had gone out with these two natives, how they had told him how to do it and set him up in a great spot, told him to put a night crawler on his hook, then

18

just cast out into the smelt and he should catch a ton of smelt!! But, "I got skunked, while they took their poles and went just out of sight upstream and filled their 5-gallon buckets in no time at all!" The native he was telling this story about his first smelting trip to told him without breaking a smile, "Your problem was you were using night crawlers; you should use just little leaf worms to catch smelt." Well, at least he knew now why he got skunked when his "buddies" caught all the fish.

It was sometime later that he heard by the grape vine that his "Yooper" fishing buddies had really set him up. He found out that when they went upstream they had some smelt nets hidden along the bank to get their fish with. The poles and worms they carried had nothing to do with it.

Our transplanted "Troll" is not sure if and when he is going to trust a "Yooper" again.

Raking Fish

The Manistique River runs right through the middle of our town down into Lake Michigan. It is great for all the locals when the fish run upstream out of the big lake into the Manistique River to spawn. When I first moved to Manistique to work, it was nothing to have dozens of people down at the river after fish with any method they could find. In the fall of the year, there were times when the river would just be full of salmon.

The Black Bass Hole sits just south of US-2 in the Manistique River. On this fall day, I was walking along the riverbank keeping to the brush looking for people after the salmon illegally. There were a good number of people in the river. I saw this party near the US-2 Bridge and saw he had a long- handled object that he was trying to get fish with. At first I thought it was a spear, but then after watching him for a while, I saw that he was not using it like a person would a spear. I came between some buildings up behind him and walked right up to him.

I stopped right behind him and looked over his shoulder. Here I saw that he had a modified rake in his hands that he was trying to spear fish with. This party had taken a yard rake and bent the points down and was trying to spear fish with it. I took hold of the rake and asked him how many tickets he would like for his little experiment. Usually if you ask a party this question they will say, "One is all I need." But this party looked me right in the eye and said, "I'll take two." I couldn't believe it, but since I didn't want to get him upset, I wrote him two tickets instead of the one I was going to write. He went in and paid the extra $50.00 and never batted an eye.

Sometimes you just cannot figure people out.

Chapter 5

Conservation Officer's Stories
Upper Michigan Tales from a Game Warden's Perspective

So You Want To Be A Writer

There is a saying; "Everyone has a book in them that they would like to write." But, what percentage ever get it out? I can guess why after all I have gone through in trying to get a book out, then trying to find a way to let people know about it.

Even some members of your family kind of look at you like you have lost it. You can tell by that look in their eyes that they thought you stayed out in the cold too long. Then, you send off a rough draft (and I mean rough) of your book and IF you hear from where you sent it, it does not do much for encouragement. You figure life is short, so why not go for it.

Putting "Your" Book Together

I tell those that ask me about writing a book, "If you feel like you should write a book, write "your" book with your own way of writing. That other person has already written with their style of writing." Now, this will get you in trouble because the "Exspurts" have their own idea what is right and how things should be done. If you have your own creative way of writing you will surely not fit into their mold. So, get ready for the letters telling you all that is wrong with the way your book is written.

I spend a lot of time talking to people that sell books and those that read a lot of books to find out what they like. They are not the "Exspurts!" but they do deal with people day in and day out. Also, talk to people from different walks of life, because you will want your books to appeal to more than one group of people. Do not be scared to listen if people are trying to point out what they feel will make your books sell better. Let me give you an example from my own travels. I had 13,000 books self-published before I realized that something was missing. With all the books I have read and all the times I have stood in stores looking at books, it never dawned on me that these 13,000 books never had anything on the back cover. When I started going to Outdoor Shows, I saw people pick up my books, turn them over to read the back, but there was nothing there. Then I talked to a party that used to publish books and he told me, "You have nineteen seconds to sell a book in a bookstore. So, one of the keys to selling it is what is on the back." The next printing I had done had the back cover filled out and it really has made a difference.

Also, find a book that has a format like you would like for your book. Then I would suggest you use a computer, so you can set it up and change things around. This is coming from a guy that has written three books on his $200.00 yard sale special. I don't know where I would ever be without it. Someday I hope to upgrade my computer so I can learn to do a few more things with it.

When you take off, believe in yourself or get off the train. If you do not believe in what you are doing, who will? The lady that owns the little paper I write for told me this after I was on the third printing of my first book and my second book was out. "John, I was scared to death when you first came in and told me that you had ordered 5,000 copies of the first printing of your first book. Nobody but the local people had ever heard of you, and I had no idea what you planned on doing." I told her, "If I didn't believe in myself, and that it would work out, it never would have. I had to believe even if nobody else did." If you know my troubles with the English language and how my daughter says, "Dad, you write everything backwards", you realize that I had to just take off running. About all a guy like myself could do was say a prayer asking for God's help and some directions from Him. Things worked out where I had over 20,000 copies self-published the first year.

Don't Quit

This is the story of my miss-adventures as I started off in the book self-publishing business. I just kept on trucking, as my wife became a basket case.

After writing all over the country and finding out that there were all kinds of people willing to publish my book, if only I would come up with five to ten thousand dollars to encourage them, I then contacted A&J Printing down in Nixa, MO, and found that they would print my books for two to three dollars a book cheaper than anybody else's offer.

All I sent them was a computer disk and the pictures I wanted in the books. The pastor from the church I attend had already laid out the book. They set the book up and sent me the proofs to look over. They were checked over and sent back, and in two days I had 5,000 books in Nixa, MO, to pick up. It is just around a thousand miles from where I live in Michigan's Upper Peninsula down to the Springfield, MO, area. So, my brother and sister-in-law that live down there (she works for A&J Printing) suggested, seeing it had been a while since we had got together, why don't they bring the books half way and meet us? We made plans to meet near Springfield, Ill.

Both crews made it all right. We had our van and a trailer, and they had a pickup with a U-haul. It had rained the whole trip down there. We met in the afternoon and got ready to switch the load of books from the U-haul trailer to my van. We opened the back of the U-haul and (there was one little catch, as the brother-in-law was pulling out of Springfield with the U-haul, they had gotten four (4") inches of rain that evening-it was flood time!) to our shock saw that the bottom layers of book boxes were wet!

We all unloaded book boxes as fast as we could. The dry boxes off the top first. Then we got down to the wet boxes. I tore all these open and started to stack the dry books out of these boxes on one side of the van and threw the wet ones up front. I ended up with around 1,800 books laying around in my van, plus the boxes of dry ones. Five thousand books come to just about two tons. We had a mess, but we kept on keeping on. I do still have a good number of books that look like somebody read them out in their duck blind during a rain storm, but the first printing was finally safe in my garage and I was in the book business.

In just over four months I was in need of the second printing of "A Deer Gets Revenge". I was a lot wiser this time, so I looked into having this shipment of books shipped up north by a trucking out-fit. I figured it out and all in all this seemed like a winner after what we had went through with the first shipment. What could go wrong?

Well, the books were printed up and loaded on a semi-truck and should be at my home in a couple of days. Three days, four days, five days, seven days, no books. I called back to A&J Printing, and they got hold of the trucking outfit they had contracted with. After a couple of more days they found my books, all on a loading dock in the Milwaukee, WI, area. It seemed that the trucking company had gotten that far, declared bankruptcy, shut down, and dumped off my books. Thank goodness, the trucking company took care of the matter, and I finally got my books a couple of weeks late. But, I kept on going.

Then, it was time for the first printing of my second book, "A Bucket of Bones". I sent the disk and pictures down, and they were printed up and boxed for me. By now I was a lot wiser by two book shipments. So, I figured thinking of that old saying, "If you want something done right, do it yourself!" Off I went with my van and a trailer to get my books myself. Besides, the wife's family lives down in that area of Missouri, so why not make it a fun weekend? Everything went great. We went as far as Madison, WI, and stayed at my boy's overnight and then on to Ozark, MO. That evening we went over to A&J Printing and picked up 5,000 copies of "A Bucket of Bones". We loaded these in my van and on my trailer.

The next morning we pulled out for the thousand-mile trip back to the U.P. We drove a couple hundred miles till we came to Rolla, MO, where we planned to stop for gas and breakfast. It looked like getting them myself was going to prove to be a winner. We had a great weekend with all the family getting together, and we were already a tenth of the way home.

After getting gas I pulled in a Hardee's to get something to eat. As I turned in I noticed that the oil light came on in the van. Now, it had never done this before. I checked as I pulled in and sure enough it would blink, then come on for a minute, then go off. GREAT!

I got out and checked the oil and looked the van over. I could find nothing wrong, but when I started it up the oil light would blink off and on. I went in, got breakfast, and told the wife and daughter we would eat on the road. I figured each time the wheels went around I would be that much closer to home when this dumb van blew up! It was too old and not in the shape body-wise where you wanted to put any money in it. So, off we went.

We made it back to Madison to my boy's, just three hundred miles from home. The next day we made it home years older and a lot grayer. I found out later the sending unit had just gone bad. I just kept on trucking.

Expect the Unexpected

I guess what really amazed me in putting a book together were those that helped me out and those that didn't. As I was making plans, I figured out where books should sell and who would be willing to give me a hand. Was I in for a shock! Some of those I figured would really be in my corner and give me a hand acted like they never knew me. It was a surprise, but one I could live with.

On the other hand there were those that never knew me or anything about me that really helped me out. I could not believe it! Those who you had never met before you walked into their business with your book gave you a chance, gave you some pointers and advice, and became a real friend. When you first take your plunge, remember this and make your plans, but be ready to expect help from the unexpected and try not to be disappointed with those that you expected help from.

But, the key is "Don't quit, believe in yourself, and keep on going."

Grandpa Brown Fishing Missouri style

Chapter 6

Conservation Officer's Stories
**Upper Michigan Tales from a Game Warden's
Perspective**

My Mom, My Dad, and Tim

If you have read either of my other two books, there can be no doubt in your mind how I felt about my parents. My Mom and Dad were special, and I feel in my heart that if all kids had parents like I had we would not have all the problems we have in this country today. Mom and Dad were not famous, basically they never left the U.P., and did nothing extra special that a lot of other parents back then did not do. They were just a Mom and Dad, the kind of parents a kid needed as he grew up.

I am writing this story to let you get to know my Mom and Dad a little. I hear over and over from my kids and others today, "We cannot afford to have kids in this day and age! Look at what things cost and how expensive it is to just make ends meet." I tell them, "My Dad could not afford kids, your Dad could not afford kids, and you cannot afford kids. The day will never come that we can afford kids without any worries. You may as well have them, love them, and enjoy them the way everybody else before you did."

My Brother Tim

Timmy came along just about ten years after I did. Tim was the youngest of the six kids in the Walker tribe. We all loved our little brother and Dad nicknamed brother Tim, "Caboose". For he always said that Tim was the end of the line, and he was.

At about eighteen months old, Tim was doing great and walking around. He was also cutting his teeth. One Sunday morning, Mom and I went to early church, so we could return home and let the rest of the kids go. Tim was still upstairs in his crib when we left.

Mom and I returned from church and came into the house. Mom asked the other kids, "Where's Tim?" She was told that he was still up in his crib. Plain as day, I can still hear Mom say, "He should be up now. Tim never sleeps this late." Mom went upstairs, and I was right behind her. When she opened the door to their bedroom, Tim's crib was off to the right against the wall. We saw that Tim was lying in his bed in convulsions. One arm and one leg were twitching, but nothing else. We could not wake him up or get him to respond at all.

Tim was rushed up to the local hospital where they worked on him and plans were made to try and get him to the big hospital in Marquette. As they were pushing him down the hall to the waiting ambulance, Tim came out of his convulsions. The doctors later told us that he had gotten high fever due to cutting his teeth and this caused him to go into convulsions which caused brain damage.

We brought Tim home just like he was a little baby again. Tim had to learn to walk and talk all over again. We all loved him and learned to help him do things.

Why am I telling this story? In all the years I was at home, and even for the years my parents were alive after I got married, I never once heard a word of complaint from Mom or Dad. Never once did I hear one of them say what a bum deal it was, or how hard it was doing things for Tim now. Tim was still part of the family, still one of us, and Mom and Dad's responsibility was to love and care for Tim like all the rest of us.

I have often wondered after I got older with a family of my own if there were ever any tears shed behind closed doors in my parents' bedroom. Maybe there were, but we kids never saw any. Our family went on as it always did-only now we had a special member.

As Tim grew older he could throw a ball like you would not believe. Mom and Dad always did things so that Tim would feel important. Even when my kids were growing up, and we went to Grandma's for Christmas, it was always Tim's job to read the names and pass out presents.

As the older boys grew up, Dad would take Tim out to deer camp with him. Dad would cut firewood, and Tim would stack it. They would spend hours doing things together. I always thought that Dad figured in years to come there would just be him and Tim at home. The one thing Dad always told us boys, "Tim can go hunting with us and be a part of things, but it would be better if he was made to feel important without teaching him to use a firearm." We did just that. Tim would go to camp and help out and talk your leg off with questions.

Dad always told Tim that someday he would be buried up at deer camp under the big oak tree across the field. Today that is where my Mom and Dad are, under the big oak tree waiting for the day that Tim can join them.

As I sit here trying to put this story into words to let you see my heart and the feeling I have for my parents, I marvel at the wisdom the two of them had back years ago in raising all of us kids along with their special one and making us all feel as one and loved by both of them.

The type of parents you are is so important, because it will affect your kids for the rest of their lives. You do not have to be college educated or someone special, just care for them and love them to death.

Just remember in your later years, it will all come back to you from them.

I guess everyone should have a brother like Tim. No matter what happens I am always his brother "Big John" as he greets me with a smile. Tim never sees my bad points, never looks at my mistakes, and just always seems to be glad to see me. If I ever need a friend to just keep me going, all I have to do is stop by and see Tim for a while in the home he stays at. I can hear it now, "Hi, John! This is my brother, "Big John!" he tells all the people in the home for the hundredth time. It just gives you that feeling that you're someone special to Tim. Growing up and living with Tim has made me, my kids, and so many other people better people just from knowing and being around him.

Over 100 lbs. Sturgeon – Taken from Indian Lake

Speared from Thompson Creek

Musky from Indian Lake

My Dad at the beach & taking picture of their catch

Chapter 7

Conservation Officer's Stories
Upper Michigan Tales from a Game Warden's Perspective

A Bow Hunter?

I just like to spend time out in the woods. I have often thought that if I was lost and had to live off what I got, I would not have this extra tire I carry around with me all the time. It would soon be gone unless red squirrels have a lot of fat grams. But my dad taught me, "The fun of hunting is just having the chance to get out there and get to enjoy the great outdoors; then if you should be lucky enough to get something it is just a bonus." I'm sure glad I feel this way.

My First Fall

I always wanted to take up-bow hunting, but with the job I had and the way we worked in the "old" days there was just not time to do it. When I retired I purchased a compound bow from a State Trooper who told me it had been broken in just right. I spent the summer practicing with it and seemed to do pretty well-at straw bales.

When fall came around, I made plans to hunt from the same blind I rifle hunt from with my bow. It is roughly 4x4 so there should be no problems. I set out some bait a couple days before I planned to start hunting, and the deer were working the area. The first evening I sat in my blind, I had to make a decision! In came an eight-point buck! I sat there wondering if I was good enough to hit it, or should I even shoot at it?

I watched this buck come in right around 4:30 a half dozen times as I sat there with my bow and never did take a shot at him. The first day of firearm deer season, I was sitting in my blind when out of the corner of my eye; right about 4:25 I saw something moving along the edge of the beaver pond. As I watched, there went my 8-point buck heading back into the deep marsh along the edge of the beaver pond. He was not going to come near my blind now that I was ready for him. I watched as he worked his way along the pond at a fast walk going to the area of the dam where he was going to cross. There was no place to get a shot at him, just flashes through the trees. I knew there was one spot, just when he would have to turn away from me to cross the dam, where there was a break in the trees. I was using my boy's rifle that has a wide-field scope, so I rested it on the front of the blind and watched for the deer to step into the scope. This opening was a long ways off, so I could watch the area and part of the woods in the scope. I saw a flash of brown, and then my 8-point buck stepped into the scope and in front of the cross hairs! I shot, and he buckled up and jumped out of sight. I got out of my blind and walked across the marsh and found my buck two jumps from where I had shot at him. Back to my bow hunt.

I finally had a nice deer come in and turn just right. I figured there could not be a better shot. I raised my bow up, or should I say I tried to raise my bow up. It hit the roof of the blind, so I could not raise it up enough to get a shot. I watched the deer and figured out how to correct this problem. The next day I carried four 2x8's into the blind raised the blind up this extra eight inches, and sat in my chair. Sure enough my problem was solved. I could raise my bow up high enough to aim at the bait down on the runway. Maybe tonight.

Sure enough later in the evening in came three deer. I waited while they checked everything out and one moved just where I would have a perfect shot. I raised my bow up, and it worked great now with the roof eight inches higher up. I set the arrow and went to draw back my bow. Slowly back, slowly, then my elbow hit the back of the blind. I was soon to realize that I have enough roof clearance now, but not enough room to draw my bow back. So, I sat and watched the deer on this evening also.

The next time out, I carried in two rough cut 2x4's and extended the front of my blind out this extra four inches. I got into my chair and sure enough everything worked just great now. I had plenty of room to operate. There was going to be meat on the table tonight!

In came some deer. They moved in behind the big hemlock, and I drew back my bow getting ready for a perfect shot when it stepped out the other side. Man! It turned while behind the hemlock and came into the open area facing me. No shot here, so I let off my bow. I sat and waited, and sure enough, a little while later the deer turned, and I had a good shot. I raised my bow up and got ready. As I went to pull it back, it would not move. No matter how hard I tried, I could not draw it back! I looked down and right away saw my problem. When I had released the bow, the jacket I had across my knees had wrapped around and through the pulleys on my compound bow. It was a mess. I managed to scare the deer away as I tried to work the jacket out of the pulleys. No deer tonight. In fact, no deer all season with my bow. But, I had a great time.

Bow With a Bear

One thing about writing these stories is that someone always wants to tell you what happened to them. Since hunters and fishermen don't lie, I only put true stories in my books. This one is from a party from Illinois I met at coffee one day.

He told me that he always wanted to go bear hunting and always wanted to get one with a bow. So, he made plans to do some fall hunting for bear. He had a party set him up with a tree stand with a bait pile a little ways off and a good bow shot.

Now, you have to remember that people from out of the area are scared to death of bear. If you live up here, you learn to live with them. For one thing, in all the time I have spent in the woods, I can count on one hand how many bear I have observed. This hunter was not too fond of bear, but he would be up in the tree safe, right?

Opening day came, our hunter was taken to his tree blind, and he climbed up in it. He then drew his bow and equipment up into the scaffold with him. Now, you have to remember that most tree scaffolds are just a little platform that you sit on when hunting, just ten to fifteen feet off the ground.

Here stood our Illinois hunter wanting to get a bear with his bow, but not wanting to be a meal for a bear. All of a sudden, he saw a flash of black, and into the bait pile walked a nice big black bear. The bear reached down into the bait pile, drew out a big chunk of bait, and dragged it right over under our hunter's tree. The bear then laid down and started chewing on the bait, while all the time keeping one eyeball looking at our hunter up in the tree.

Mr. Bear finished up this chunk of bait and wandered back towards the bait pile. Our hunter had a perfect shot, so he pulled up, took aim right behind the front shoulder of the bear, and for the life of him he could not draw his bow back! No matter how he tried, he was just so tense that his muscles would not work to draw back the bow. AND here comes Mr. Bear again! Dragging back another chunk of bait under our hunter's tree! Now, our hunter is sure the bear knows he is there and is just waiting to use him for dessert. Here sits Mr. Bear now watching our hunter as he eats on this hunk of raw meat. For some reason, our hunter no longer cares if he gets a bear with a bow. He only wants to live long enough to get back to work next week. As our hunter stands there, back and forth goes our bear from the bait pile to the tree. It is finally getting dark, and our hunter feels he has another problem. How do you tell where a black bear is in the dark?

Finally, he thinks the bear has wandered off. He waits a little while and figures it is now time to head out or be the final course for the bear. He lowers his bow and equipment down to the ground and starts down the tree. He makes it to the ground and hears a grunt off in the ferns. His feet are on solid ground and he is going to grab his bow and make a run for his car!

Our hunter reached down, grabbed his bow, and took off running down the trail for his car as fast as his legs would carry him!! Running wide open about twenty-five feet from the tree his feet go straight out from under him and he crashes into the trees!

It seems that in his rush to escape and live through this bear hunting trip, when he hit the ground, heard the grunt off in the ferns, grabbed his bow, and took off running, in his rush. he forgot to untie the rope that he had tied to his scaffold to lower his bow to the ground. Nobody has any idea where the bear ended up.

A Maine Deer Drag

This story comes from a Maine Game Warden. The only thing is, those strange people we call "Trolls", the people in Maine call "Flatlanders". I just figure that Eino and Teivo must have cousins that live out that way.

It seems that this Maine Game Warden was out working deer hunters one day. He had walked back into the woods quite a ways and came across this crew of hunters. Our Game Warden knew right away that these two hunters were "flatlanders", and they had gotten a deer and were dragging it out.

As our Game Warden walked up to these two hunters, he saw our two "flatlanders" were trying to drag the deer they had shot out to their car by the tail! Here were these two hunters both trying to hang onto this little short deer tail and drag this 200-pound buck out to the road.

The Game Warden checked out the two hunters and found the deer was tagged legally and everything was in order. He then suggested to our two "flatlanders", that it might be a little easier to each grab one of the buck antlers and try dragging the deer out to their car this way, by pulling on the antlers.

After standing there and thinking it out for a minute, our two "flatlanders" agreed. Even though they agreed that it might be easier pulling this big buck that way, there was still one problem! They told our Game Warden, "If we were to grab the buck by the antlers and drag it that way, pulling it by the antlers, we would be dragging it away from our car instead of towards it!" What could the Game Warden say? He had tried to help them out.

U.P. kids hauling in the big ones

Chapter 8

Conservation Officer's Stories
Upper Michigan Tales from a Game Warden's Perspective

Yooper Kids

Did you ever sit, think back, and wonder how you ever lived through your growing up years? When I was doing this as a teenager, there were times that being an average teenager; you never spent too much time thinking. As my saying goes, "A teenager thinking can be a dangerous thing to behold." But, maybe, sometimes, it would not hurt just to try thinking just a little bit.

One of my mom's favorite sayings when we "felt" sick and were moping around the house was, "Get outside-the fresh air will make you feel a whole lot better." It did not matter if it was twenty below zero! It must have worked because I cannot remember us kids ever being really sick. Here are some stories about the younger years. Now remember, a lot of this was before TV ruined our lives when kids still did everything outdoors.

Trapping-Kids' Style

I have told people a number of times about the importance of trapping when I was a kid. It was just something Dad always did. The story goes, and I have stated it before, that I was paid for with just one beaver hide when I was born back in 1943. This hide sold for enough to pay all the doctor and hospital bills back then. So, trapping was a way of spending a boy's Saturday afternoon.

We would get our gear and snowshoes to go up the Norwich Road to look for some active beaver dams. Our project was to snowshoe back to the areas where we hunted along the old railroad grades and set some beaver traps. This was the period before anyone ever heard of snowmachines. We would make out beaver sets using a stake on the bank. Attached to the stake was a long wire that either went to another stake out in the water or an object under the water to make a drowned set. The beaver would get caught in the trap, and then nature would tell him to dive down into the water. You had a piece of metal that slid along the wire to let the beaver dive in, but he couldn't return to the surface. Then, you had him.

A couple of days later we would run our trap line and look over our sets. Most of the time if you had caught a beaver you could usually get him to shore by working your slide along the wire or pulling the stake driven in out of the water. Once in a while, this would not work. Here you stood with a nice beaver at the far end of your wire that you could not reach. No matter what you did you could not recover your trap. Back in those days we never heard of waders, so to say the least we did not own any. There was only one thing you could do. The lucky party got to sit on their snowshoes, remove their boots, socks, and clothes to go wading into this ice water to recover their trap and beaver. It was always a "hold-your-breath-turn-blue" type move. When you had recovered your trap you got to experience the true feeling of being freeze dried. Because all you could do was rub yourself dry and get back into your clothes.

The funny thing is none of us ever got sick from doing this. In fact, I cannot even remember us catching colds. Maybe it was that greenish-brown bottle that sat in the fridge with the slimmy greenish-yellow stuff in it that you drank back then if you got sick. Cod-liver-oil!

I have often wondered what my dad did when he ran into problems trapping? He never owned any waders either.

Bum's Camp

Back when I was growing up, the main way of hauling freight was the train. Almost every good-sized town had a railroad and a train that ran into it. What went right along with this was an area back in the woods just outside of town called "The Bum's Camp". A lot of the old lumberjacks would hop a train car to get from town to town. Most of them never had any place to stay when they arrived in a new place, so they just jumped off at the "Bum's Camp" and slept under the stars.

Well, it was every youth's dream back then to hop a freight out of town and travel to places you could only dream of. Usually if you did hop a train you stayed on only long enough to get the feel of it and to get a couple of miles from town. Then you would jump off and return home. These guys had the life! Travel where you wanted, do whatever you wanted, and not a care in the world. Not even any school to worry about.

One weekend a couple of us boys decided to try out the lifestyle of living at the "Bum's Camp". By this time there were fewer and fewer bums traveling by train. So, off we went with packsacks, sleeping bags, some food and a tarp. We went over the tracks to the "bum's camp" and set up camp. We had the whole place to ourselves. We were right on the bank of the Ontonagon River in the spring of the year when the water was really high and fast. We set up our tarp tent and horse played around. In the evening we built a nice fire to cook supper and keep the ghost of bums past out of camp for this night. We were having a ball with nobody to give us any unwanted advice or tell us what to do. As it got later, we made plans to call it a night and crawled into our sleeping bags.

I had the job of putting the fire out so it would not take off in the dry leaves during the night. Being on the bank of the river, I figured (a teenager thinking can be dangerous) the easiest way to put the fire out was to push it over the bank into the river. I took the side of my foot, placed it next to the fire, and pushed as hard and as fast as I could sending the fire through the air into the river just like I planned!! The only problem was along with the fire went my shoe!

Now, you have to remember that back in those days you had "A" pair of shoes. This pair of shoes was for play, for school, and for church on Sunday. In fact, I cannot remember having more then one pair of good shoes at a time till I got in the service.

So, here I stood on the bank of the river with one shoe on and one shoe off down in the muddy water of the river. I cannot swim a lick, and I had to get my shoe back or else hop around on one foot the rest of my life. There was no way I was going to return home without both shoes. In the middle of the night, in the middle of nowhere, a teenager that could not swim lowered himself over the bank of the river into the muddy, ice-cold, fast-moving water to feel around on the bottom for his missing shoe. I was out in the slimy red clay water up to my neck trying to find my shoe. (It never dawned on this teenager that maybe mom and dad would rather have a one-shoed live teenager then no teenager at all.) I could not find it and had to return to shore a couple of times to recover from the cold water. Finally on about the third or fourth trip out hanging onto a tree branch I felt my shoe on the bottom! I managed to work it around till I could recover it.

I sit here now more scared than I was that night almost fifty years ago wondering how many Guardian Angels a Yooper teenager goes through growing up in the backwoods.

Youth Wisdom

This story fits right in with the last story. As a youth, you were always out on these adventure trips with your buddies. Life was always interesting back then because you were always lucky enough to find something to make it that way.

On this sunny, warm spring afternoon, we had gone for a walk up the railroad tracks. We had crossed over US-45 and worked our way along the tracks for a couple of miles. We had found a lot of junk and gotten tired of just poking along the tracks, so we headed back for town. As we were coming into the area of US-45 again, we saw all the junk sitting around the county garage. Now, nobody had ever told us not to play there, so this must mean that it was open season to monkey around the county garage area. (If you have not been warned not to do something, being a normal Yooper boy, it could only mean it was all right to do it. This has to be true, because by the time you become a teenager, you have been told not to do almost everything that you figured out was worth doing. Right?)

Here we are on this warm, sunny, spring day. It was beautiful out. We climbed all over everything and played with all the things worth playing with when we came across this area that proved to be great. There was this spot behind the garage where the sun had warmed up this liquid on the ground. We found that if you got back and took a run, you could slide for a long ways, just like on ice in the winter, only better. We had a ball.

I had more trouble with shoes growing up. This pair was what you called "boondockers" after the war. You could buy them for a boy that was always out in the woods getting into everything and they seemed to last a while. On this day I had on my boondockers and was having a ball sliding in this slime. (You have to remember that being a normal boy I was always getting into trouble, because a boy had to check out every water hole to and from school. Therefore, you were always oiling or treating your boots to make them waterproof.)

On this day, as we slid around in the slime, I noticed that this stuff seemed to work real great at waterproofing my boondockers. Hey! I had an idea (danger lurked)! Why not take a stick and treat my boots all over with this waterproofing? After all it was the same color as my boots. So we did.

Finally the fun of something new wore off, so we headed back toward our homes. I returned home just knowing my parents would be so proud of me. I had solved the problem of waterproofing boots forever.

As I entered the house, I was stopped dead in my tracks! When asked where we had been, before I could even explain the good deal I had found, I was shipped back out the door. When asked who, how, what, and where, I was soon to find out I had blown another one.

It seems that this great fun spot we had found was the tar pit for the county garage! On this warm spring day the tar had warmed up just enough to make it slimy and fun for us boys. The theory was good on the waterproofing, but somehow the results were not.

Do you know how long it takes a boy with a can of gas and a rag to clean off all the tar from his boots? This, after things had started out looking so positive.

Dock at the cabin on Lake of the Clouds
Porcupine Mountain.

Our big catch

Chapter 9

Conservation Officer's Stories
Upper Michigan Tales from a Game Warden's Perspective

Something Stinks!

Well, when you live in the backwoods there is always something that will get your attention. It may be with the aid of the kids, the family dog, or just one of your lucky days. These are a couple of the crazy things that people ran into during their trip through life.

'Shut-up"

I guess if anything really bugs a person it is when there are dogs barking as you try to sleep at night. It does not really matter if the dogs belong to you or someone else. Once you hear them, you are doomed, and there is no way you are ever going back to sleep till you get them to quiet down. What makes it all the worse is when it's one of those hot muggy summer nights when all the windows in the house are open, and it sounds like the dogs are right in the bedroom with you.

This was one of those warm, muggy summer nights. This party that was trying to sleep had a couple of hunting beagles that had a place right behind the house. Usually these dogs are really well behaved, and you would never know he even owned dogs when you stopped by. BUT! On this night, for some reason, both beagles really cut loose in the middle of the night. Sure enough, it finally woke up both the husband and his wife. After listening to them for a while, hoping they would stop and let them go back to sleep, the owner got up went to the back door and yelled at them to quiet down!

They did quiet down. For about as long as it took him to get back into bed. Just as he got comfortable and rolled over to doze off, both beagles cut loose again!

This went on two or three times-the dogs barking, the owner crawling out of bed, going to the back door, yelling at them, the dogs quieting down, the owner crawling back into bed, and the dogs cutting loose again. To top it off, remember this was one of those hot muggy nights when all the windows in the house were open, so there was no hiding from the noise.

Finally, enough was enough! The owner pulled on his pants, slipped into his shoes, and went out to settle the dogs down! Out the back door, grabbing a broom as he exited the house, across the yard to the dog run. Here he yells at the dogs to get into their house and quiet down. He threatens them both with the house broom! The dogs, fearing for their lives and not knowing what to do, make a beeline for their doghouse! BUT! Our owner finds out real soon that the beagles' house was already occupied-by a skunk! This was the reason the dogs were out in the yard barking and acting funny in the first place. In the doghouse stood Mr. Skunk, standing up for his rights, because it was his house now!

Picture this, these poor beagles. They run for their lives from the owner with a broom into their doghouse. Mr. Skunk who is now in charge of the doghouse lets fly at the beagles, so they tear back out of the doghouse only to see the owner standing out there with the broom. Back into the doghouse, only to find Mr. Skunk again. This circus went on a number of times so fast that it did not compute with anyone.

Finally, Mr. Skunk got tired of defending a home that was not really his after all and moved off into the night. But, it seemed he did not take everything he had brought with him. The smell was so bad in the yard that everyone about died. The dogs were covered with it and whining now, and remember that all the windows in the house were open, which meant no sleep for sure tonight. Except for Mr. Skunk that is who had wandered off to find a quieter home.

Lucky Mom

You have to realize that if you lived where there was a river running right through the middle of town, there would be some interesting times. This is the case in Manistique.

In the 1960's the state of Michigan started planting Coho salmon in the Great Lakes for sport fishermen to catch. These salmon live most of the year out in the big lake, but at spawning time they run upstream into the creeks and rivers to spawn. When this happens, some of these rivers are literally full of fish. It made for some interesting times for the Game Warden-and also for Mom.

After school or on weekends, it was a mass exodus down to the river for the kids. It was a great place to catch fish, build rafts, and plain old get wet and dirty. They could also catch all the fish they wanted and then some. The only problem Mom had was with the younger kids who did not understand all the finer points of fishing.

You see, when these Coho salmon came up the river to spawn, they never returned to the big lake. They slowly died as they spawned in the river. Now, picture this. Here comes this younger fisherman with stars in his eyes about catching one of these big fish. He goes down to the river and tries at first to catch one hook and line without much luck. The fish are all over in the river, and you can watch them since the water is only inches deep in a lot of places. No luck with the fishing pole, but maybe there is another way.

Our little fisherman goes out into the water, tennis, clothes and all, to try and catch a fish. He herds them around till he works one over into the shallow water on the rocks. Now's his chance! He does a belly flop onto the half rotten body of the biggest fish he ever saw. There is a wrestling match, and after a fierce battle, our little fisherman wins. He thinks.

Off he goes, heading for home, with a smile from ear to ear, bear-hugging this rotten fish for Mom to see. Into the house, through the back door, into the kitchen, with a yell, "Mom, come see what I caught!" Mom comes into the kitchen and about dies! She is not sure what stinks the most now, her boy or his fish. Mom, in her wisdom, tells the young fisherman, "That's just what I've been looking for to bury in my flower garden to help the flowers grow." Off the boy goes to bury his prize catch happy that he was able to be such a help to Mom as he hears, "Take off ALL your clothes on the back steps I'm running some bath water, so you can get cleaned up as soon as you're done burying your fish."

Before Plastic Buckets

Did you ever stop and think how tough life was before these 5-gallon plastic buckets came along? Nowadays, we use them for everything. trash cans, apple buckets, bait buckets, water buckets, life is so simple now. BUT! back when I was a kid......

I was sitting one day recalling one of my adventures as a teenager going smelt fishing. First of all, don't bother to try to tell people that live in other parts of the country what smelt are, because they will never understand. How can you explain that we take hand nets and go out to fill buckets, pickup trucks, trash cans, or anything that will hold them full of smelt? You usually do this at night, and then you return home and spend all the next day cleaning those you are not lucky enough to give away. You take a pair of scissors, cut their belly open, run your thumb through, and that's it. You may want to cut their head off, but some people do not bother. You eat these fish bones and all, and they are great to eat when fresh out of the lake.

But, some of us teenagers made plans to go out to Patty's Creek to do some smelt fishing. We rounded up a net, got some warm clothes, but could not find anything to hold the smelt we were going to catch. We looked all over without any luck. Then I got to thinking, I should have known in the long run this could not be good.

My dad had a number of milk cans that he kept for taking fresh water up to the cabin. Why not? I could use these and later wash them out and Dad, who was at work, would never know. Off we went to Patty's Creek where the smelt were running. We managed to dip enough to fill all the milk cans we had. Boy, were we lucky!

We returned home and spent the next day cleaning fish. After we were done, I took the hose and cleaned out the milk cans real good, and I just knew that Dad would never be the wiser. A couple of days later Dad was to take a trip up to the cabin, so he filled a couple of the milk cans with water and off he went.

When he returned home I knew right away he was not a happy camper. For some reason, unknown to me, he did not like fish flavored coffee. After a short question and answer period, it was plain to Dad what had taken place. For some reason all the food I had supplied for the family did not seem to cancel out fish-flavored water. (Now, these metal milk cans are about a 5-gallon all-metal can with a metal lid that were used to take milk from the farm to the local dairy back in the Stone Ages.)

I spent days using everything they made back then from bleach to scouring powder to SOS pads trying to get the fish taste out of

Dad's milk (water) cans for the shack. NO luck. I think years later when I left to go into the service if you stopped by our hunting cabin you could still enjoy a cup of fish-flavored coffee with us.

A Strange Smell

I was out on patrol one day checking the area along Lake Michigan. It was a nice warm summer day before any of the hunting seasons opened up. In the area I was working there was a lot of undeveloped land back then. (It sure is not that way ten years later!) There were a lot of deer and other animals that roamed the area. Also, a good number of ponds for waterfowl and fur-bearers could be found.

I came around a curve, and there was a pickup truck parked on the side of the road, the wrong side of the road. I pulled up facing the truck, not really expecting to find much, because right in this area there was nothing but a bunch of sand dunes. But, why not check it out? I talked to the two men in the truck, then I checked the firearms they had plus their hunting licenses. Everything I checked seemed to be all right. They told me they were just out enjoying things, not really up to anything.

As I stood by the truck talking to these two men, I could smell something. I should know that smell! It had a real distinct smell that I should know, but I could not for the life of me figure out what it was. I knew I should know what it was, but I could not place it. I killed time talking to them, all the time poking around the truck trying to place this sweet, musky smell. What was it? I should know.

I must have spent fifteen or twenty minutes looking around finding nothing that could be putting off this distinct smell. They had nothing I could see that would be producing the odor. I checked the inside of the truck, the junk in the back of the truck, but there was nowhere it could be coming from. Still, it was there. I went through things for about the third time looking for the cause of this foreign smell. I moved everything around again-even the waders lying against the cab in the box of the truck. This time I picked the waders all the way up and found they felt heavier than they should have. I turned them upside down to see what was in them and out fell a couple of fresh beaver pelts. I knew I should have known what caused that smell! Now I knew I did. 49

Needless to say, it was not beaver season.

The King of the lake caught on a pink lure by a lady...
...The poor husband.
43 1/2 inches - 22 1/2 pounds.

Chapter 10

Conservation Officer's Stories
Upper Michigan Tales from a Game Warden's Perspective

Passing Them On

As you get to telling stories there is always someone that has one of their own or maybe even a better one. Since I have written my two other books people from all over the country send me their "favorite Game Warden story". These are a couple of stories that I had a chance to hear. I did not make them up, they are not mine, but they are interesting.

My mother's family comes from Tomahawk, Wisconsin where part of this story takes place. In fact, I have to wonder at times if at the end they may have been in Uncle Bill's place. I am told that the story came from a Len Schmitt from Merrill, WI. I just felt you would enjoy it, so I'm passing it on just as it was sent to me, grammar and all.

Justice Prevails

As district attorney, I was prosecuting a man by the name of Emil Gutsdorf for illegal possession of beaver hides. The warden's testimony was, and they established that they knew, that he was at a beaver pond at a dead end road up in the northern part of Lincoln County. They parked their car where the dead end road joined the main highway and waited for him to come out. Finally, pretty much after dark around 9 or 10 o'clock at night, Emil came out with his old Ford, and he had a man sitting on the front seat with him. As he pulled onto the main highway and turned toward Tomahawk, the wardens pulled up behind him and followed him. It was raining very heavy, and as they pulled alongside of him and flashed their light in his face, he just kept speeding up and speeding up, and they kept telling him to stop, but he just kept going and the man in the front seat turned down the window and threw a bundle out the window. The warden yelled, "Let's go back and get the package—we know that it's Emil Gutsdorf and we'll get him later." So they went back and they picked up the package in the ditch, and, sure enough, it contained three illegal beaver hides.

So now we had our trail. Emil had had twelve previous convictions for game law violations, so he did not take the witness stand on his own behalf. He put up a weak alibi. We were able to break it down so completely, that it appeared that the jury would only be out a few minutes. They went out at 2:00, and everybody expected them to be right back. But they didn't come back, and they didn't come back. The eminent Judge Reid had an important speech at Wausau that night before a church group and was confronted with the choice of declaring a mistrial or missing his appointment. But he was so sure Emil was guilty that he didn't want to let the case go, so he cancelled his speech and stayed there.

Finally, at about midnight, the jury dragged in and found Emil guilty. As I was walking home, I got about a block from the courthouse and the jury foreman caught up with me. He was a little laundry man in Merrill, and he said, " Len, I bet you wonder what happened to us and what took so long." And I said, "Yes, I did." And he says, "Well, we were 11 to 1 for conviction right off the bat, and we didn't even sit down at the table, but there was one juror who said he was a neighbor of this defendant and he wouldn't vote guilty and he kept holding out and he says my neighbor wouldn't do anything like that, and he held out and held out. It got to be past 11:00 at night and a couple of big Dutch farmers from the town of Corning grabbed him, and one got hold of one shoulder and one the other and they rattled his head up against the stone wall of the jury room a couple of times and they said, "Look, neighbor or no neighbor, this man is guilty and we're going out of here now with a unanimous verdict of guilty and you're going with us' and the fella finally saw the light and went along, and the jury returned the verdict." And he says, "I don't know if I should tell you all this." I said, "Well forget it Bill." So anyway Emil was sentenced to one year in prison then because of his previous convictions.

About two years later, I was up in Tomahawk at noon and went to a tavern where they served sandwiches; I walked up to the bar and ordered a sandwich. Emil jumped up from a card table and came up to me, and said, "I bet you don't know who I am" and I says "Oh yes I do - you're Emil Gutsdorf." He says, "that's right," and he kind of smiles and says, "You know you gave me a rap once but I forgot that. To show you I'm a good fellow let me buy you a drink." I says, "Well, alright, Emil, I don't mind if I do have a drink with you." I added, "By the way, Emil, that neighbor of yours almost saved you that time. He held out 'til the very end." And Emil says, "Neighbor, nothing, Len! That's the man who threw the furs out of the car window!!"

(The backwoods English and grammar in this story was left just the way the story was given to me.)

Only at Christmas

If you are a Game Warden, one thing you hate to have happen is to have a jury trial right before Christmas. It seems that no matter how many times the party you are going to trial with has been caught before, at Christmas time the jury is just in a forgiving mood. If you can work it out till January when the same people are getting all the bills from things they charged for Christmas your chances of winning are a lot better.

This is one of those stories of a just-before-Christmas jury trial.

It seems that this party was caught cold with an illegal deer after season. He was caught with a fresh deer out in the woods, so there was no way for him to get out of it, except maybe with a jury trial. So, he asked for one. He had a number of things going for him. Number one was that he was one of these big old friendly guys that everybody likes always had a big smile and a story for everybody. Also, he had a rather large family, and everybody in town knew he could use the meat, and it would surely not go to waste.

The jury trial came along, and the case was laid out. In fact, it was pretty cut and dried. The officers had caught this party out in the woods dragging out a freshly killed deer after season. There was really no denying it. In fact, the party never even took the stand to try and put up an alibi.

The case went to the jury with our deer shooter's only chance being the Christmas Spirit here in the backwoods this time of year. We all knew that he had a better than 50-50 chance of winning. The jury was out for quite some time and finally returned to the courtroom with a verdict.

The jury foreman stood up and stated they found him guilty of taking a deer out of season, but with circumstances. The judge announced he accepted their verdict of guilty and found the man guilty and asked what were the circumstances.

The jury foreman stood up and said, "Your honor, we know the party is guilty; there is no way from what we have been told he could not be. So, we had to find him guilty, but we feel seeing the time of year it is and that this man has a large family to feed, we want to pass the hat to help pay off his fine, so he can be home with his family for Christmas." As he finished, he reached down on the floor for his hat.

Around the courtroom went the hat for all to place something in it, even the judge, to take care of the fine of our had-to-be-found-guilty deer shooter.

Gordon Gunther was one of finest Christian men I have come to meet in my travels as a Game Warden

The wife and me at my retirement party (Blaney Park Inn)

Our District won the Regional Match even with me on the team

Thanks Cliff for making my boy's day

Mike from Crosscut Cafe

A great morning

Sturgeon caught from Indian Lake

Musky displayed at Mobile station in Paradise

A paraducks

*Nice
catch!*

I love it here

Flat on my back enjoying life

A perfect day with my dog

Waiting on just the right moment

Early morning along an inland lake

One of our best duck hunting spots

Looking out over Lake Michigan along US-2

Looking out over Lake Michigan from Skyline Restaurant

Fall in God's Country

What a great place to live!

Looking out over the Big Lake

Sunset over Manistique Lighthouse on Lake Michigan

Sunset over Lake Michigan

Chapter 11

Conservation Officer's Stories
Upper Michigan Tales from a Game Warden's Perspective

My Opinion

I thought I would take this time to include a couple of articles I ran in my newspaper "column". I guess I am just scared of the way the "rights" of hunters and fishermen are going and how fast they are getting run over. I don't care if you agree with my stand or not, we are all losing out. This letter was sent out in the winter of '95.

To: Department of Natural Resources Commission

From: John A. Walker, Outdoor Writer, Author

Subject: Outlawing of deer and bear baiting

I sit here trying to keep a cool head in order to write you this letter without getting upset.

It sure seems kind of ironic that the same week that the DNR Wildlife Division came out with a proposal to outlaw deer baiting there were state-wide survey results carried in the paper stating how fed up people of Michigan were with state employees and their attitudes.

It appears from the feedback collected in this survey that state employees no longer listen to or care about the people of the state. They just want to promote their own programs and forget the tax-payers and what they may like to see.

I would like to point out the following facts:

1) In the years since hunting from blinds and baiting has become popular, the number of hunting accidents have dropped drastically. This information comes from the DNR records. A party sitting in a blind hunting over bait with a clear shooting lane should never mistake another hunter for a deer.

2) I have taught Hunter Safety for around thirty years, and each year I see more and more girls and ladies attending classes.

Why? Because they can enjoy sitting in a blind watching deer come and go even if they never really care if they actually ever shoot one. For years, I have taken kids out with me to sit in my blind to watch deer.

3) If we are not careful, Law Division of the DNR is going to play right into the anti-hunters' hands. Each year they cry about all the problems they have with hunters during hunting season. Let me make two points here:

    (a) There have always been problems with hunters out in the field, or else why have Conservation Officers? Thirty years ago when I worked the Thumb Area, we had problems with hunters feuding over who should hunt where and whose deer it was. Problems with this many people in the field all at once is nothing new, only some of the new DNR employees seem to think it is.

    (b) Stop and think a minute. I have written about this in a number of newspaper articles, and I think the DNR needs to understand this fact. Where else could you get three-quarter of a million people out in the woods for a two-week period and have as few problems as there are percentage-wise? Let Michigan, Michigan State, the Lions or Pistons win something and read about the number of arrests that night of those partying. With the number of hunters there are in Michigan there are bound to be some jerks out there that have no respect for the rights of others or the laws. BUT! Please don't paint all of us hunters with the same brush. Just be thankful that 99.9 percent of us hunters behave and enjoy our hunting from our blinds over bait piles and do not bother anyone.

4) I think most of us agree that it is silly for hunters to go out on public land and dump a truckload of bait along a road and hunt over it. Since I have had 23,000 of my two books on the outdoors self-published in the first year, I have received hundreds of letters from hunters and non-hunters, which gives me a feeling for what they think from what they say in their letters. I cannot recall one person that would find a problem with stopping baiting within a couple hundred feet of a public road. Most of us that walk back

into our blinds take a 5-gallon bucket as we go in to sit. Most real hunters could not get a truck into their blinds to dump it.

5) Some of us that hunt from blinds over bait get a deer some years, but other years we get "skunked". Being retired, I go out and sit almost every day. There have been years I have not seen a buck, but I sure do enjoy being out there waiting for deer to come in. You would have to hunt for the pure enjoyment of hunting to see what I mean. Getting a deer does not make my season: the enjoyment of the outdoors does. So many people are truly missing something important about the sporting side of hunting.

In closing, I hope you will stop and think about what Wildlife Division is asking you to do and why? Please, do not take away from us the enjoyment of taking kids out to a deer blind with the snow blowing in the cold weather so they can see deer come into a bait pile. If you do, you will be starting a trend toward the end of hunting enjoyment and, maybe the end of hunting down the road.

Also, please do not use what happened up at Seney this fall as an excuse. Don't listen to the Lieutenant from the District. Talk to some of the family involved and the officers in the field, and you may be surprised to find this had nothing to do with hunting at all. There were a lot of people and newspapers that jumped to a conclusion before all the facts were in.

Please, allow us to continue to bait.

Sincerely;
Retired Conservation Officer and Outdoor Writer
Sgt. John A. Walker

Attn: Governor
Rep. Gagliardi
Senator North

Fish Report: 1-9-95

Well, I guess I should finish what I started last week. I told you that I would try to explain how in this country we are now passing laws backwards. It was never meant to be handled the way it is today in our state or nation. This is going to be hard to explain in a report the size of a weekly Fish Report. In fact, you could teach a whole lesson on it.

First, let me say that I have always enjoyed history. In fact, my two boys majored in history in college. Also, if you were to look in the World Book Encyclopedia, you would read where Salem, MA. Was settled in 1626 by the relatives of my Grandma Theiler. So, we have been around just about since it all began, the setting up of laws for our country, that is. We have sold our birthright, and I have to wonder if we will ever get it back.

Let me point out something that is being run backwards which is the cause of a lot of the crazy so-called "laws" we have. Our system was set up where the "people" elected people to speak for them in the state or federal legislature. The two bodies that make up the legislature were meant to pass the laws to control those that did not fit into the system. THIS IS THE KEY! Laws were never meant to be heaped on the shoulders of honest people and businesses.

Let's start at the beginning for most of us. Almost all of us were taught a few things when we were little: (1) Do not steal (2) Do not murder, and so it went. Now, this is the key. Most of these laws if obeyed, do not affect us. They are there, but hopefully, they will never affect us. They are there for the-law breakers, those that steal, those that murder, etc. They do not put an added burden on the lives of honest citizens. This is what laws were meant to be, a system to control the law-breakers, not to control the honest people.

So, what happened? The legislature we elected to control the law-breakers has turned the system right around and is controlling the honest people, and the outlaws are running all over us. They do this in two ways.

Think about this. A good percentage of what we call laws now, because they have the power of laws, are not even passed by the legislature. Years back, our elected officials were either too scared or too lazy to take the responsibility for passing the laws like they were supposed to, so they passed it on to other, non-elected, agencies. This is a responsibility they had no right to give away, because under our system, if we, the people, do not like the job these law-passing officials are doing we can vote them out of

58

office. We CANNOT vote these departments or agencies out of office.

Example: Before the election last fall, a party came by my home and asked me to vote for the re-election of our state representative. I asked her, "You tell me why I should after the legislature just passed a law where I have to now register my snowmobile twice to take a ride out on Indian Lake?" I held them responsible for their actions. This is how it was meant to be. But, not today.

Our legislators, both state and federal, have sold our birthright, and now we are all paying for it without the proper checks and balances.

Example: Some clowns take an ORV and go out and tear up the countryside, destroying everything they come across. So, what happens?

An agency passes a rule, without the vote of our elected legislator; to outlaw the use of ORV's by everybody, including the honest people. This was not meant to be our system. The laws were always there to control those that were wrecking our natural resources, why not use these? No, it is just easier for an agency to outlaw the honest legal use of the resource by everybody.

Example: You get a small percentage of hunters that have to make problems during the firearm deer season. Across the whole U.P. with all the hunters out there, there were only 492 tickets issued. Of these, 22 were for illegal possession, 30 were for shining, 156 were for firearm violations (the largest category). There were only 23 tickets issued for so-called blind violations. Twenty-three out of how many thousand hunters in the U.P., and this is a problem!

In fact the largest District in the U.P. had zero (0) blind violations! Where is the problem they keep claiming is there?

They say, "Let's pass another backwards law, not by our elected legislature, but by an agency to control all the thousands of honest, law abiding citizens out there exercising their honest rights as citizens of this country. Let's outlaw baiting for deer for everybody, instead of stopping those that are abusing the privilege.

Example: The EPA says there are problems lying on the bottom of our river. The EPA, one of these agencies that passes its own rules, says "you and you" did it without needing any proof beyond their opinion. When departments and agencies have been given this type of power, that they were never meant to have, we are all in trouble.

In closing, I want to point something out and hope you can understand what I am trying to say in this short space, because its hard to do. Maybe, you do not like baiting for deer, maybe you do not like riding an ORV back into a trout stream to catch a few fish, maybe you do not like to just sit in a deer blind with your daughter and watch for deer, but what you do like may be next on some agency's hit list. You may well wish you had helped us out when we had our battle.

Remember the Bingo problems of the 50's? Remember when they were going to pass rules against Potlucks at churches? What is next? Is it something you like to do? Lets get our system back to what it was supposed to be. Let's allow the legislature to pass laws to control those that are harming our nation and let those that love our nation and enjoy it keep having the chance to enjoy it. Then, every couple of years, we get to vote on the job these elected officials are doing. We cannot do this with the system we have now.

This is the third part of "My Opinion" about getting involved when someone is stepping on your hunting or fishing rights.

Fish Report: 1-29-95

Well, it sure is nice now that spring is here. But, I just have a feeling that I may get to move a little snow yet this year.

They are getting a few nice perch out on Indian Lake. Not many, but those they are catching are nice.

Well, I sit here wondering if I ought to go out in the back yard and kick the fire out of the tree planted back there. There is a story to this. A doctor told my dad one time, "Art, you keep too many things inside. Get mad once in a while. Go outside and kick the bark off a tree once in a while." I guess I am at that point.

As you know I have written a number of articles about the hearings on deer hunting that are going on throughout the state. I have to take time to comment on these. The more I read and hear about these hearings and the plans for them, the worse I feel.

First off, I received a letter from the DNR at the governor's request telling me about the hearings. This was great, but then the joke came in the next line that went something like this, "We are planning on ONE hearing in the U.P. and will allow about "3-minutes" for those that would like to make a comment." What a joke! A person who wants to try to express his feelings on this issue is going to be blessed with "3-minutes" to do it in. I have to wonder if the special interest groups that call on the DNR are only allowed three minutes to speak. I find that hard to believe. It makes a person wonder, after having watched our governor a couple of times in the last month on C-span, how he would feel after going to Washington to "speak out" on what he believes if he was told, "Go ahead, you have 3-minutes to do it in." I find it hard to believe he would like it.

Second, the DNR tells us they are going around to get the "people's" input at these hearings. I have to wonder about that when I read in the Escanaba paper on Friday what their opinion already is! It seems like their mind is already made up. As is the Forest Service who did not even have the character to hold a public hearing. How can the leaders of the DNR expect people to be a part of their programs and support them when they are treated like this? If you want people's help, treat them like they are adults, please.

I have talked to hundreds of people and groups during my time and asked them why they don't get involved with the system? I have received the same answer dozens of times. "Why get involved? They usually have their mind already made up before they ever hold a public hearing. It is just a waste of time! The only reason they even do it is so they can say they gave the public a chance to respond. They never listen to the average man on the street." You have to wonder if these people are right.

For your information, there is a feeling throughout the state that certain people within the DNR and Forest Service simply want to outlaw baiting for deer and bear. For this reason, they have gone out of their way to collect every thread of evidence to support their personal feelings. In fact, after the hearings were ordered, they were still trying to collect facts to support their ideas. The feedback I get from people in a number of law enforcement agencies is that many of the so-called "baiting conflicts" had nothing to do with baiting at all. I was told they would have happened anyway!

Third, I would like to ask those in public office who saw what happened last November when it appears that people stated with their vote that they wanted smaller government in the hands of the state, to carry it one step farther. How about letting it go from the Washington level to the state, but don't stop there, from the state to the average citizen? Is it wrong for the pulp cutter from the U.P. or a person from a little U.P. town to want to be heard? Then, please, take time to honestly listen to what they have to say.

Fourth, I was always taught, "You can designate authority, but you cannot designate responsibility!" If you have read my whole series of articles on this issue, you know what I mean. We can be told, "The stinking DNR or Forest Service passed that law." BUT! Who let them do it? Those we elected! Remember that the DNR Commission is appointed by the governor! The DNR Director serves at both their requests! I find it kind of ironic that someone from the Natural Resource Commission has to get up and even state, "We are not anti-hunting." I sure hope not, or we are all in trouble.

Let me end with this food for thought, which fits right in after reading Friday's article. Some jerks on ORV's do damage to state or federal forest lands, so they outlaw all of us from using them. A person cannot even "putt" back into a trout stream and catch a few fish. BUT!! Two years later the forestry section from either one of these groups bids out the timber on the same section of forest you were stopped from operating your ORV on, and the loggers take skidders, dozers, and tree farmers back in the same area and just flat tear up everything! Do all these, "let's outlaw everybody from everything laws" we are seeing passed all over now really make any sense? Maybe I'm getting old, but they don't to me!

(Copies of all of the articles I wrote on this went to the Governor, Rep. Gagliardi, Senator North, and Congressman Stupak. For some reason, I never received a reply from any of them. I wonder?)

Membership Card No. 2 52

ONTONAGON SPORTSMEN'S CLUB
NORTHERN MICHIGAN SPORTSMEN'S ASS'N

Date 5-1-38

Received Of _Jerome Walker_

DUES TO 5-15-39 , 50c

Lyle Rockman

Sec-Treas

Officers with illegal gill nets

Chapter 12

Conservation Officer's Stories
Upper Michigan Tales from a Game Warden's Perspective

The Fawn

In the picture section of my first book, A Deer Gets Revenge, there is a set of three pictures of a fawn that was killed illegally. I get asked all the time about these pictures. They were put in the book to show what a great job the Michigan State Police crime lab can do in assisting a game warden in his work. After getting asked the story about these pictures so often, I guess I should tell it.

One day during the month of August, I received a call from a party that there were the parts of a spotted fawn in one of the green trash boxes up at the intersection of M-94 and Thunder Lake Road. I picked up my partner who was stationed here at the time, and we took the twenty-mile trip up to check the complaint out.

We came to the green trash boxes and looked inside. Here, we found the head, hide, and a few other parts of a spotted fawn. We figured, "Great, something, but really nothing so far." We moved the parts around and came across a bunch of school papers that had the names of the kids on them. All were from the same family. We gathered all this evidence and did some more work on getting our facts from the complaint and what we had seized together.

We then went to the local court system and got a search warrant for the family business and home of the names found on the school papers. With a State Trooper to help us out, we made the return trip up M-94 to the little town of Stuben to carry out the search warrant. During the execution of the search warrant, we recovered dozens and dozens of packages of frozen venison from the freezer in this little store. At this time of year, it was illegal to possess venison without a permit. We seized all our evidence and made plans for going to court. We knew with this case we would end up in court.

We sat down and tried to figure out how we could tie all this evidence together. We had the fawn parts from the green trash boxes and the packages of frozen meat from the store. I got to thinking. I had worked on a number of timber stealing cases where the crime lab had matched the butt of a log to a tree stump. Why not see if they could match the fawn head to the neck roast from the store. We marked all the evidence and took the neck roast and the fawn head up to the crime lab. Sure enough, they were able to take the neck bone from the fawn head and the neck bone from the roast from the freezer and make a perfect match. In fact, they were able to make a slide show to show the jury just how both these pieces of evidence came from one and the same deer.

We got ready and went to court. We had a pretty good case, we thought. We had the people charged with possession of an illegally killed fawn and possession of venison out of season. All this evidence was placed before the jury, and the men from the crime lab did a great job with their pictures and slide show. It went as smoothly as could be. Then the jury went out and returned a while later.

They found them "Not Guilty" of possession of an illegally killed fawn! We could not believe it! There was no season open, and they had the fawn in their possession! But, Not Guilty.

They did find them guilty of possession of venison without a permit. My partner was new on the job and fit to be tied. I told him, "Just hang on there. This judge we have has been through the mill. Don't worry, he knows what went on." The young officer could not be convinced, but there was nothing we could do.

A week later we returned to the courthouse for the judge to sentence the party that owned the store. The party stood up before this backwoods judge figuring he had gotten away with something. Then, the judge dropped the roof down on him, along with the courthouse and the whole block of buildings. The judge later told me that he always felt it was the biggest fine anyone up to that time had ever received for having some venison out of season without a permit.

Sometimes the scales of justice do balance out. You just have to wait a while for it to happen.

Chapter 13

Conservation Officer's Stories
Upper Michigan Tales from a Game Warden's Perspective

Fishing as a youth

Well, I guess that I had two of the best grandpas a boy could ever have. My dad's dad was confined to bed as long as I knew him with cancer, but he still knew how to make a boy feel good and make him neat things with his jackknife. My mom's dad was always there getting us kids into trouble or teasing us about something. You could never really figure out where the line was between truth and grandpa pulling your leg. It was just a way of life back then. This is one of those tales that got you thinking.

Wooden Boats

Back when I was a kid, there were few families that even owned a boat. Of those that did, they owned a big old wooden boat that took two men and a boy to even move around. Metal boats were not to be found back then. Of course, my grandpa had a boat.

In fact, my grandpa made a few wooden boats. It was neat to see how they made the ribs, put it all together, and then molded the wood to bend it in place to form the bow of the boat. It was a project. During the winter there were always the times you had to sand down your boat, patch up any bad spots, then repaint the boat to get it ready for the next fishing season.

Come the spring of the year, Grandpa would take the boat, place it on a trailer he had made, and haul it down to the lake. You would then wrestle it into the water and watch it fill halfway full of water! I could not believe it! All that work all winter in the garage, and the boat has as much water in it as the lake does! Grandpa would laugh and say, "Don't worry, it's supposed to do that. You have to allow the water to get into the boat before you can expect the boat to keep the water out." I would stand there looking at the boat half full of water wondering on which side of the line grandpa was standing. Was there truth in this, or was he pulling my leg again?

A couple days later we would make another trip down to the lake to his water-filled boat. It still held water pretty good! We would take a coffee can and bail the water out of the boat till we could roll it up on its side and dump what was left out. Grandpa then said, "Watch this and you may learn something." We would lower the boat back down and push it out in the water as I stood there and watched and could not believe what I wasn't seeing! I watched and watched waiting for the water to run back into the boat, but it did not. I stood there as a youth dumbfounded as Grandpa laughed and told me what had happened.

He said, "Son, when we first placed the wooden boat back in the water, it was all dried out from sitting in the warm garage all winter. This is why the water came in through the cracks. But, after a couple days in the water (both in and outside) the wood swelled up and plugged the cracks closing the leaks up. Now it floats and keeps the water on the outside where it belongs."

I stood there figuring I had about the smartest grandpa a boy could ever have.

Strange Hours

Well, as a youth there were a number of things that were pretty cut and dried in your life. Going to school and getting the best marks you could was one of them. It was not what you would call a multiple-choice question. Back in the olden days, when I was a kid, one thing that you were quick to learn was that bedtime was at a set time. Early. You were told that you could not learn without the proper amount of sleep.

This was one of those things that was set in cement. That is until a certain time of the year rolled around. It seems that when the spring rains came with the warmer weather there was a distinct change in the attitudes of most dads. As a youth you had to wonder sometimes, but you sure did not complain about it.

As the warm weather came and the water temperatures warmed up it, was time to go check the creeks that ran into the Great Lakes for smelt. These little fish, for some strange reason, seem to like to try and sneak into the streams under the cover of darkness, and then for the most part, return to the big lakes before daylight. When this happened, it meant that a person had to leave home about 9:30 or 10:00 at night and head out to the creek mouth to wait and see if the smelt would run tonight. Even on school days!

Off you would go with your hand-nets and buckets to head for the beach. There would always be a number of large bonfires burning to keep the lookers warm. You would stand around these and listen to the adults talk or run around and horse play. Every once in a while a party would take their nets and go down into the creek to take a couple of dips and see if the smelt were running yet. The thing that amazed me, as a youth was that there were never any clocks when out looking for smelt. It was just an accepted fact that smelt ran at night, sometimes the later at night the better. It was about the only time of the year that the rules of getting to bed early so you could get up for school the next day were waived. Maybe there was no scientific reason for a boy getting to stay up till the early morning hours looking for smelt, but who was I to complain.

You were soon to learn that it was only a special treat, because as soon as you had lucked out and got the smelt you wanted, your staying up late nights were over. Then it was off to bed at the appointed time each night no matter what.

I think back through the years and wonder at my Dad's wisdom to take me down to Patty's Creek looking for smelt. I could never really figure out why my Dad thought getting wet and cold along with a few smelt, if we had any luck, was so important. My Dad did not even care about fishing that much. But, as I look back after all these years, I think of how my Dad used it to build up a rapport between the two of us. The going after smelt was not the reason, it was to show that dad cared about the little things that his boy cared about. If it was important to me to go smelting like the rest of the kids did, it was worth the effort for my dad to see that we got to go.

Years later when I had to make important decisions in my life affecting my family, or me I would always give dad a call for his input. Maybe it was just the need of a security blanket from someone who you respected, but it was still needed. I think back now and am sure thankful for those nights around a fire out looking for smelt when dad built up this special relationship. Thanks, Dad.

Yooper Prowlers

If you live in the U.P., you had better be ready!

On a night after a good warm rain, about an hour after dark, there could be strange things happening around your house. If you are new to the area you may think there are creatures poking around your house. About an hour after dark you will see two or three lights moving around your yard. These lights will be hovering just a short ways off the ground going around and around in little circles. They will stop once in a while in one spot then move off again around your whole yard. There are spots where the lights may move slower than other places, but they are sure to be there. If you were to look real close in the area of these lights you could spot a little pair of tennies. Then, you may spot the reflection of an old coffee can. Now, this only takes place after a hard rain, usually in the early summer. Could it be the haunts of the Yoopers past?

No, it is just a way of life for a youth in the U.P. who likes to fish. After a good warm rain, he gets his buddies, a flashlight, and a can, and then he goes out to pick night crawlers for fishing. There is some real skill involved in being good at this trade of night crawler picking. After the rain, the night crawlers are forced to the surface in the grass. They come up after dark to lie there. They stretch out always keeping one end back in the hole. You move around bent over with your light just a little off the ground trying to spot a crawler. When you do, you set the can down and quickly reach for the end of the crawler nearest the hole. If you guess wrong, you come up empty.

The key to really testing your skills as a night crawler picker is when you get a chance at a "double". This is where Ralph comes up to the surface and moves over to visit Hazel next door. There Ralph sits whispering in Hazel's ear, both with the far end still in their holes in case they need to make a swift retreat! You would set down your can, place the flashlight between your legs and try to get Ralph with one hand and Hazel with the other. It was big time when you got a number of "doubles" during the night.

Back when I was a youth you would paint a little sign and sell night crawlers for 25 cents a dozen. It made for BIG bucks back in those days.

Chapter 14

Conservation Officer's Stories
Upper Michigan Tales from a Game Warden's Perspective

Lucky Fishermen

When you spend twenty-five years working as a Game Warden, you sure run into some interesting things in your travels. I don't care how many things you see or hear, there are always a few that really stick in your mind. I am going to try and relate a few of the different, but true, things that I came across. Really, you have to place yourself in the stories to really get the true feeling for each tale.

A Matter of Life and Death

As I have already stated a number of times, the Manistique River runs right through the center of our town. After school the kids are known to make a beeline for the river to get some fishing in. On this day there were a number of brothers and friends down at the river. As usual, there were some fish in the river, and everybody was doing their best to catch one. Not always are the methods used the ones you see on those fishing shows on TV. It is usually cast out, jerk your line, reel a couple of turns, give another jerk, a few more turns of the reel, another jerk, etc. This is the type of action that a lot of kids use to get fish.

This afternoon the kids were doing their best to catch some fish. This one boy pulls back, whips his pole as hard as he can to make a cast to the far side of the river. Only something goes wrong, and he realizes his hook never hits the water! He hears a yell, and right away knows where his hook is. Stuck in his brother! And he did a good job of it, too. Try as they might, they cannot get the barbed hook out of his brother's body. There is only one thing to do, grab the pole and head for home, brother, hook, and all. They tear into the house that sits only a couple hundred feet from the river yelling for help.

Here comes mom to the rescue. They look over this poor hooked boy that could be scarred for life from this afternoon of fishing with his brother. Both mom and dad settle their nerves and settle down to try to get the hook out of their son's body. But again, try as they might, they cannot get the hook loose. Mom makes a call up to the local hospital to tell them to get ready in the emergency room for they will be bringing their son up with a fish hook embedded in his body.

They take a towel and wrap it around the fishhook to hold it in place, and then they transport their son to the emergency room to try and save him from being forever scarred. They place him in the car and head up to the hospital and around back to the emergency room entrance. The doctor has been called, and everything is ready for when they arrived. The boy is rushed in as the mother explains that they all tried to remove the hook, but could not get it out. They lay the boy out on the table and make ready for maybe "major" surgery. They slowly and carefully start to remove the towel that has stabilized the fishhook for the trip to the hospital. As they get it unwrapped and slowly pull it away from the area where the fishhook is embedded, they look, and there is no fishhook! They could not believe it. The fish lure is gone!

They all stand there dumbfounded looking at a couple of holes where the fishhook had been. Then, the doctor looks the towel over, and sure enough, here is the fish lure now firmly attached to the towel. It had worked its way out on the trip from home to the hospital.

By the way, the fishhook was stuck in his foot.

| A Special Person Checked |

(When wrong can only be right)

In all the hours I spent through the years checking fishermen out on the lakes, there is one time that I have never forgotten. For two reasons. First of all, on this opening day for pike and walleye, we decided to patrol Indian Lake. It was in the afternoon and a really nice day with a good number of fishermen out on the lake. For the only time I can recall this ever taking place, on this day it seemed like every boat we checked had caught fish! Not just one fish, but each member of the crew in the boat had a real good day.

We checked a good number of boats and worked our way up towards the north end of the lake, still seeing good catches of perch, pike, and walleye. As we entered the bay near Big Springs, there were a number of boats fishing there. We checked a few and then pulled up to this boat with a father and son in it. We soon found that this was about the only boat in all those we checked so far that day that had not caught a fish.

We talked to the dad as he was helping his boy who appeared to be in his early teens fish. Everything about them seemed to be legal, and we were just visiting for a minute before we pulled away.

All of a sudden the boy let out a yell, "I got something!" The dad told him to settle down and just take his time and let the fish tire itself out. The boy played the fish as Dad coached him and helped him a little till the fish was up next to the boat. The dad quickly reached over the side and flipped a pike that was on the boy's line into the bottom of the boat. The boy was doing everything but dancing as the fish flopped around in the bottom of the boat. He kept telling us that it was the first fish he had ever hooked and caught all by himself. Dad settled his boy down and told him he would take the fish off the hook.

Dad removed the fish as the boy's eyes just sparkled. Dad then said, "We had better check your fish to see how long it is to make sure we can keep it." The boy gave his dad a look when he told him, "to see if we can keep it." Dad got a ruler out and measured the pike, and it came up to about 18 1/2 inches no matter how you tried to measure it. Dad tried to explain to his son that a pike to keep had to be 20 inches long.

The son couldn't understand this, and I'm not even sure he could understand what the difference between 18 1/2 and 20 inches was. All he could understand was that this was the first fish he had ever caught, and he was a teenager. He was about to shed a tear as Dad tried to explain things to him.

Having grown up with one, I knew right away that this teenage boy was one of those special children some parents are blessed with. He was not real bad, so he could do things with Dad. But Dad's day on the lake was spending 90% of his time helping his mentally handicapped boy out.

I looked at the dad and said, "I'll tell you what. One 18 1/2 inch pike is not going to make a whole lot of difference in a lake this size. A lot of dads that had a son like yours would not even spend the opening day of pike and walleye season out helping him fish. Go ahead and let him keep his first fish, and we're glad he caught it."

I'll tell you what! Money could not pay for the smile and look that lit up the face of that boy and his dad out on the lake that day. The dad still told us that they would release it like they were supposed to, and he would try to explain it to his son. Both the old Game Wardens told him to forget it. Some things in this world are just right to do even when they may seem wrong.

Some People Have a hard Time Changing

There is this little guy that goes to the church I attend that can really tell a war story about the Game Wardens. (They must all be true, because he tells them to all the teenage boys at church.) I know for a fact that some of his stories are true because I have been around long enough to have heard them from other people. But, this guy turned over a new leaf. In fact, one day he told me a story that proved it to me.

He told me the story like this. One day, the night before the opening of bass season, our little buddy was out fishing. As luck would have it he hooked what he knew right away was a really nice fish. Now you have to understand that at this time of the year everything you catch in Michigan the season is open on except....

He is standing on the shore playing this fish that he knows is a dandy. Slowly but surely he plays the fish out and works it over to where he can get at it. He pulls it in, and it is the biggest bass he has ever caught or for that matter ever seen caught. He looks at the fish, and looks at his watch, and looks at the fish, and looks at his watch.. Guess what is the only fish in the whole state of Michigan that the season does not open till tomorrow on? You guessed it, bass!

He told me he thought of a dozen different ways he could figure out from times gone by to make sure this fish could be caught legally the next day. Tie it to a tree, sit and look at it for twenty-four hours all the time planning to release it till season opened, and you wouldn't have to, etc.

He then told me, "John, I thought about it and about you and Dale, and there was no way I could look at you next Sunday if I kept that bass. So I just unhooked it, picked it up and gave it a big hug, and bent over and released it back into the lake. John, do you know how hard that was for me to do?"

Mom! Get the frying pan ready!

Chapter 15

Conservation Officer's Stories
Upper Michigan Tales from a Game Warden's Perspective

A Game Warden's True Skills

I thought I would take a few lines and let you read about some of the real "skillful" cases that Game Wardens I know have come up with. After reading them, you will have to admit they are rather interesting.

You Better Get There Quick!

Some officers don't even know their own skills. On this night, late at night, an officer received a call that there was some deer-poaching going on. He knew that in the area where the complaint came from, it was a known fact every December when the deer migrated through the area there was poaching.

So, he jumped out of bed knowing he had to get there quick! He did not even bother to get dressed, but just grabbed his issued snowmobile suit that was lying over a chair and pulled it on over his BVD's. He slipped on his boots, and out the door he went. He covered the ten or twelve miles to the area of the complaint and watched for a minute with his lights out. Sure enough, here came a car down the road shining the fields with a spotlight trying to locate deer. Our officer pulled the car over, and there were a number of people in both the front seat and the back. He seized the spotlight and a gun and told them to head for the State Police Post, and he would follow them.

When they all arrived out in front of the post, the officer walked up and told them all to get out of their car and head in the post. He noticed then that the guys in the back seat seemed to be rather on the large side coming almost to the roof of the car. Out they piled to walk into the post. As the two guys climbed out of the back seat, the officer noticed they were not overly huge, in fact on the small side. So, he shined his flashlight in the back seat and almost fell over!

Here, in the back seat of the car that our two poachers had been sitting in, lay two deer that they had already shot before the officer reached the area of the complaint. He could not believe his skill at catching them. What was it? Not taking the time to get dressed before he headed out on the complaint, of course.

In fact, after he herded them all into the Post, the Sergeant sitting behind the desk suggested he ought to zip up the snowmobile legs and front seeing all he was wearing did not hide a whole lot.

Just the Right Timing

One night, we had been out working fish spearers for about four hours and had not found a thing. We had checked a number of fishermen, but they were all legal. We knew the pike were running and there would be those after them, but we had never been in the right place at the right time to do any good. So, we decided to take a break, as we weren't doing any good out here.

We left the area where the poachers were supposed to be after the fish and headed down the highway to an all night gas station restaurant for a cup of coffee. We were figuring it was just going to be a wasted night.

We came around the curve and were pulling into the restaurant when we observed a group of guys stationed in front of the gas station under the lights. We looked closer, and here was this one party standing there as big as life holding up a stringer of big pike he had just speared! Seeing pike season was not open at this time of year, we figured just maybe this was not going to be a wasted night after all. And it wasn't.

I guess it just goes to show that sometimes a cup of coffee gets you more than working does, but don't try to convince the boss of that.

Good Eyes

On this night, I was working with an officer from the county north of me. We had been working both the fall fish runs and trying to find some shiners without much luck. The area where we were working was as flat as could be, so you usually just parked your car and waited for someone to come to you. There were no hills in the county to sit on and watch a large area.

After a pretty dull night, we decided to stop a while and have a cup of coffee. It was the type of full moon night that you could almost see as well as you could in the daylight. We had just pulled over and parked when we saw this car coming towards us. We stood and watched as it drove right by us and went on. I yelled, "Curt! There's a gun laying on the roof of that car!"

We threw our stuff in the patrol car and took off after this car, pulling it over. Sure enough here lay a loaded firearm on the roof of the car. The driver was dumbfounded. But, he did say it was his gun. It seems that he had spotlighted a deer standing out in a field and took out his gun and took a shot at it. He then laid his rifle on the roof of his car and walked out to see if he had dropped the deer. He had missed. So, he rushed back to his car and took off wanting to get out of the area where he had fired the shot. In doing so, he drove right by us. So, we seized his firearm and wrote him a ticket. Boy, we sure had found a different one tonight.

Not all is well, because it doesn't end well! The judge found him "not guilty" because he knew this boy and could not believe he would ever do a thing like shoot at a deer at night!

Bird Watchers

There was this one officer who if he sold luck would have made a million dollars. On this day, he was driving down a highway that runs through a deeryard. He was not really doing anything this Sunday afternoon but putting miles on his patrol car. As he was going through the deeryard in an area we call the S-curves, a party ran out in the road and flagged him down.

They told him they had been back in the woods watching birds, and a couple of guys had just shot a deer back there. The officer went back in the woods and came up with the deer, but the party took off running. So, he had the illegally killed deer, but no bodies.

He figured the case was gone seeing he could not come up with who had killed the deer. He thanked the people who had helped him out, loaded the deer, and headed into town. He told a few of the people he worked with how close he had come to catching these two guys that had killed a deer up on the S-curves. But, he had missed them. Case Closed.

A couple of days later, one of the local Fire Officers who liked to work with the Game Wardens and was always a law enforcement officer at heart, was sitting in a local restaurant having a cup of coffee. Over at the next table was a group of young guys talking. One of the parties was telling his buddies how lucky he and his cousin had been last Sunday afternoon. They had been up in the deeryard on the S-curves and shot a big deer. Just after they shot it, they heard the Game Warden coming and ran back into the deeryard and got away.

The Fire Officer called the Game Warden that had already figured his case was gone and told him what he had overheard at coffee. They went to the local prosecutor and told him both half stories that now should make a whole case. It did, and warrants were issued for both cousins.

The Shoe's on the Other Foot

On this night, there were a couple of officers out working pike spearers. It was a real project back then in the spring of the year. The few nights the pike ran heavy in the area, the officers worked a lot of hours both day and night. We worked seven days a week back then when the action was there.

On this night, about a week into the fish runs, these two officers were on patrol together. They knew an area where there should be some activity. They drove over that way and checked for tire tracks that led off the main road back into the area where the pike spawned down a dead end road. It was really hard to get back into this area and surprise the poachers, so the two officers figured they had a better idea. Plus, they were tired after all the hours they had been working.

They checked the tracks over good to make sure that there was only one set going back down the dead end road. Only one set. So, they figured the outlaws had to drive back out this way, because the creek was over two miles back down this dead end road. There was no other way out. They parked their patrol car blocking the road and sat back to wait for the poachers to come out. They figured they would see the headlights of their car in time to get out and surprise them. As they waited, they talked for a while then just sat back to watch.

All of a sudden, someone was beating on the roof of their patrol car, and they about jumped out of their skin! The driver rolled his window down, and the party standing next to the patrol car asked, "Would you mind moving your car so we can please get by?"

Guess who it was! Needless to say, there was no use checking them, for our two officers had both dozed off.

Thank You Kindly

This night, we had a group patrol with the airplane helping us to spot shiners. Back at this time, you could shine all night if you wanted to. You could even have certain firearms with you while shining if they were locked in the trunk of the car. BUT, you could not have a center fire rifle or a shotgun with buckshot or slugs.

On this patrol I was working the Cooks area near some of the potato farms. We had stopped and checked a number of vehicles out shining but had not run into any violating. The officer from the plane called and told us he had a vehicle shining over off M-149 near Big Springs. We worked our way over in that direction as the plane kept an eye on the shiner. We came up behind the vehicle that the plane told us had been shining without our lights on. We stopped and watched to see what they were going to do. They pulled down the road a ways, and sure enough, they started shining again, so we came flying up behind them turning on our spotlights and blue light to pull them over. They went a little ways and pulled over to the side of the road.

We got out to check them out, and when I spotted the driver, I knew right away this crew was not out shining for just fun. We got them all out of the car and checked it over good, but could not find a firearm.

At this time the officer in the airplane directed my partner back to the area where the car had been stopped along the side of the road. As the officer looked around, he found a high-powered rifle lying in the ditch. He returned up to where I was standing with the crew of shiners, and we asked who owned the rifle. "Rifle! What rifle? It is not any of ours!" We had not seen them toss the rifle out, so there was no way we could say it was theirs.

I asked them once again if they owned this rifle all the time thinking we had messed up this one. As we were talking, I took my flashlight and looked the rifle over. I ABOUT DIED!! Right in front of the forearm, engraved on the barrel was a driver's license number!

"All right, everybody back here. Let's see some driver's licenses from all of you." Guess what? We made a match and made our case.

Another Gift

Once again, we were working with the aid of an airplane, but this time north of Gulliver. In this area there are a lot of deer that move through the fields. I was sitting with my partner and watching for cars shining. It was a real quiet night. After a while, we decided to move from one area to another and maybe change our luck.

We were driving down River Road when we came to a real sharp curve. Right when we got halfway around the curve, we saw this car headlighting right in front of us. Before we could do anything, doors flew open and bodies went running everywhere. By the time we realized what was taking place, we had nothing but footprints and a vehicle.

We got out to look around not really knowing if and what they might have been doing wrong. It was not illegal to be driving down River Road this time of night. All the bodies had gone running off into the woods on my left. I got thinking; if they all went running off to the passenger side of their car, why not check the area off to the driver's side. I walked back into a little opening where there is a small cemetery and about tripped over a firearm laying there in a gun case.

I went back to the patrol car and started adding everything up and came up with zero! We had a car that we could find out who owned, but we could not put the owner in it. We had a firearm, but who's to say who it belongs to? We did not see who threw it, and rifles cannot be traced. I figured, oh well, at least it broke up a dull night.

I then went to check the firearm out and place it in the trunk. As I turned the case over to unzip it, guess what I found? A hunting license pinned to the gun case. Now, at least I had a body to go looking for. We found him.

You have to remember, "To transport a firearm in an area frequented by wild game you need to have a hunting license" in Michigan. This man surely did not want to be out there without his hunting license, therefore breaking the law. By the way, other than during firearm deer season, it is illegal to transport a centerfire rifle after sunset in a game area, and this was not the firearm deer season.

BILL THELER'S TAVERN
HOME OF THE WORLD'S LARGEST
FISH POLE
TOMAHAWK, WIS.

WIS. CON. DEPT. PHOTO

My uncle Bill's pole

Chapter 16

Conservation Officer's Stories
Upper Michigan Tales from a Game Warden's Perspective

I Wish I Hadn't Done That

I guess we all at one time or another do or say something that we wish, when we see the results that we had not done. These are just a number of short little items that I have run across where, if the party had it all to do over again, he may have handled it just a little differently.

A Hurtin' Pinky

As I have stated in a number of my stories, I like to spend time in the fall of the year out bow hunting. I am not really good at it; in fact I may be what you would call bad at it, so I tend to pick the brain of those that have been more successful.

On this day, I asked this fellow officer, who is a good bow hunter, if he used a tracking string. He said, "Used to." Then he told me these stories.

One day, he was up in his bow stand (in a tree) watching over his bait pile. A short time later a deer came into the area, and he watched it as it worked its way around to the area of his bait. He waited till he figured he had a good shot and took his time, pulled back, aimed just where he wanted the arrow to hit and let fly. Just when he released his arrow, he stated, it felt like his little finger on his left hand was on fire and burning off!

As he got control of himself, (he never said if he hit the deer) he looked at his little pinky, which was now covered with blood and about cut through and realized what had happened. It seemed as he pulled back, aimed at the deer, and got ready to release his arrow, his tracking string somehow got wrapped around his little finger.

It made me, a future bow hunter, wonder.

Another Day

This time another bow hunter was up in his tree stand waiting for a deer to come in. As he stood there looking around, he spotted a deer off to his right. He watched as the deer walked closer coming right into the area where he would have a perfect shot. He waited till it stepped right into the spot he wanted, and then he pulled back on his bow, took a perfect aim, and released his arrow. He watched the flight of his arrow toward the deer. BUT! About two feet from the deer it seemed like his arrow stopped in midair, in mid-flight, and fell to the ground scaring the deer off. The tracking string had gotten caught up as it was unwinding from the spool. No deer today.

Strange Sounds

Have you ever been there? You get all ready to spend a fun afternoon out on the lake. It could be the party out fishing or the game warden out checking fishermen. You go and pick up your boat and get all your gear together. Off you go down to the river to the boat launch.

You back your boat up to the launch, get all your gear out of your truck and place it in the boat, check to make sure you have everything lifejackets, radio, ticket book, flashlight, coffee, etc. You go around the back of the boat and take the tie downs off the boat and are ready to back it in. You back it up alongside the dock back into the water. When the boat floats off the trailer, you get out, walk out on the dock, pull the boat back and over and tie it to the dock. It is now time to get back in the car, pull it away from the launch and park it, so off you go.

After parking your vehicle, you walk back to the boat ready for a good time out on the lake. As you stand on the dock getting ready to jump into the boat, you hear this strange bubbling sound. Now, you had never heard that before, what could it be? You look around and all of a sudden realize that the back of the boat is sitting way lower in the water, and all your gear that you had loaded in the boat is now floating around in the bottom of the boat!!

Then a light comes on in your head, and you realize that the strange noise you hear is water coming into the boat thru the plug hole!! You forgot to put the plug back in after you drained the water out of the boat last time.

Now, what!? Should you try to get the plug back in before the boat settles to the bottom or make a run for the truck and try to get it backed to the boat before it goes under. Sometimes a person just has a bad day.

Silence is Golden

Being a game warden up here along the Great Lakes makes for some interesting trips. It is nothing to get in your patrol boat and travel forty or fifty miles or more out on the lake. (As I stated in one of my other books, you would have to take time to look at and realize how big the Great Lakes really are.)

Today there was a group of officers working out on Lake Superior. They had received complaints that there were some commercial fishermen from Canada coming into Michigan waters to catch fish. Out on the water, it is a real project to try and catch them when they are doing this. There are two reasons. Number one: out on the open water you can see objects a long ways off, and then they would make a run for the border. Number two: most of your commercial tugs now are equipped with radar, so they can spot a patrol unit coming long before you get close to them. For this reason, there is usually a lot of planning that goes into one of these illegal commercial fishing patrols.

You usually try to keep track of where they are fishing illegally with the aid of the patrol plane. Then you want to make sure they are far enough from the U.S.-Canada border that you can intercept them before they can cross back over. Sometimes it works, sometimes it doesn't.

On this raid, they made plans to give chase to the illegal tugs if they came over far enough into Michigan waters. Off the officers went trying to head them off at the pass, so to speak. They succeeded in catching them before they made it back to the border, and one of the Michigan officers jumped from his patrol boat onto the illegal gill net tug. But, it still would not stop. The officer had to figure something out and fast, so he yelled, "This is kidnapping! Besides being charged with illegal fishing in Michigan waters, you'll be charged with kidnapping TOO!! For taking me with you! If you don't stop this boat right now!!"

These Canadian commercial fishermen did not want to get in any more trouble than they were already in if they got stopped. They figured there was only one way to get out of the kidnapping charge. So, they picked up the conservation officer who had jumped on their tug and threw him over the side out into the middle of Lake Superior!

At a time like this, as you hit the always ice cold water of Lake Superior, two things go through your mind, "I wish I hadn't said that!" and "I sure hope I have some buddies in those patrol boats."

Inconsiderate Farmer

When I first started as a Michigan Conservation Officer, we drove our own cars out on patrol. A short time later, we were issued state patrol units.

This one night, I was out working shiners in the farm country that had a lot of wood lots in it. There were a lot of deer in this area. As usual, you did 90% of your night patrolling back then with your lights out. But, you had worked this area so many times before that you knew where each road, fence line and lane was. If you were driving down the road and saw headlights come towards you, you would just find a place to duck in and wait to see what the car was doing.

Here we were driving down this gravel road without a light on trying to spot another vehicle. All of a sudden, we saw headlights turn off a side road and come towards us. It was late enough at night that normal people should be home in bed, so every vehicle you figured was a good possibility. This car was a lot closer than we figured, so we had to back up fast to get out of sight. BUT, I knew right where there was a fence lane behind us to duck into. I stopped quick, put my brand new patrol car in reverse and backed up at a good clip. I came to the edge of the field where the lane was and cut it hard to get into it. We made it-almost!

It seems that since the last time I was here this inconsiderate farmer that owned this piece of land had decided to park one of his plow units in the lane, right next to the road, under the back of my brand new patrol car.

You Lied!

I was always told this story over and over about an officer that was just a real guy, but for some reason, he caused a lot of stories.

On this day, they were out on patrol checking hunters. They came up to a crew of pheasant hunters standing along a county road. The officers got out to check them out and make sure they all had their hunting license. They all checked out all right and the officers were talking to them when one of the officers noticed a firearm lying in a car. He asked, "Is this firearm loaded?" He was told it was not, so the officer raised the firearm up to take it out of the car. As he was still removing it from the car, the barrel was pointed up, and he somehow managed to pull the trigger. Guess what!! The gun was loaded, or should I say the gun was no longer loaded. But, how about that car?

But It Hurts

I was driving along a back road one day when I came across this party who was out trapping. Now, we all know that all sportsmen like to show off any new toys they have. This trapper was no different. As we stood there talking he just had to show me the new "jump" traps he had just bought.

Here we stood at the back of his pickup talking as he was showing me how great these new traps worked. He bent over, placed the trap on the tailgate, opened the jaws, and went to set the release trigger. BAM!! All of a sudden the trap slipped and sprang up catching all four of his fingers on one hand in the trap. He didn't know if he wanted to laugh or cry at that minute. Me, deep down I wanted to say, "That really worked great, but I would have just taken your word for it. You didn't really have to stick your hand in it to prove it to me."

How Am I Going to Explain This?

One day I was out checking fishermen along a little stream that runs into Lake Michigan. I pulled up into a little 2-track to hide my car. My plan was to walk back along the creek looking for fishermen. Before I could do this, I had to catch up on my paperwork!! If all else fails, you have to do your paperwork. After all, there are at least a zillion jobs in Lansing that depend on all the paperwork produced in the field to justify their jobs! So, I had to do it.

I shut off the car and turned the switch over to accessory, so I could listen to the radio and catch up on my paperwork. I got caught up and got out of the car to walk down the creek to do what I was paid to do, catch bad guys (not fill out forms). I walked around for an hour or more and did not find anybody worth checking, so I headed back to the car. Just as I walked over a hill and spotted the patrol car, a light came on in my head, and I thought, "I didn't." But, when I got to the patrol car and checked, I had. There hung my only set of keys still in the switch. In these new patrol units there is no way you can get into them either, unless you want to break out a window. Now, they don't even have the little vent windows to break out. If you break one it has to be a BIG one. There was no way I wanted to do this. It would mean another ton of paperwork trying to explain what happened to the window.

I figured I might as well walk down the beach as I cooled off and tried to figure out what to do. I did say a little prayer asking the Good Lord to help me out of this mess. I came to a place where a party had camped and had a fire on the beach. Here I found an old lawn chair with a metal part on it. This I took back to the patrol car and managed to work in alongside the door and get it unlocked.

For once, I got out of doing some of that paperwork that Lansing needs so badly.

Maybe I Shouldn't Have Said That!

Another officer and I were working out at Thompson Creek looking for people after the trout. We parked our car and walked into the area of the fish weir. As we came out of the trees, we saw a number of three-wheelers parked at the weir. They were not supposed to operate motor vehicles in this area. As we walked through the opening up to the weir one party jumped on his three-wheeler and took off. We yelled at him, but off he went.

We talked to the other youth and found out they were not able to operate ORV's. We told them to go with us back to where our car was parked. As we came along a 2-track trail here sat the party that had run off from us. He decided to hide right by the patrol unit; not realizing it was even there. I asked him why he had run off and not stopped when we yelled. He told us, "My dad told me never to stop for a cop; just take off running and let them catch you if they can." We had.

After what happened, we made out tickets and seized the three-wheelers seeing they could not even operate them legally. They asked us what was going to happen to their ORV's? I looked right at them and said, "We take them right over to Turek's junk yard! Men only ride Suzuki and these are Honda's." Not thinking, we left it at that and went on our way. We took their ORV's up to our storage garage and placed them in it.

A couple days later I returned home after being out on patrol, and my wife said, "You had two calls from the court, a couple from some parents, and Turek's called wanting to know about the three-wheelers they were supposed to have!" I said, "AAAAAAAH!

U.P. Library

Chapter 17

Conservation Officer's Stories
Upper Michigan Tales from a Game Warden's Perspective

A True Friend

I have always said that those that are anti-hunting have never really had the pleasure of having the kind of friendships built around hunting together. It is more than just the actual act of just getting something. It is the fun you have being together, laughing, and wanting to have someone else succeed rather than just yourself. I know, because I have come across and built these type of friendships through the years. Here are a couple of stories about hunting friends.

But, It Was My Boy

As I have stated many times in the stories I have written, I have two boys. If I get the chance, I sure enjoy going out hunting with them. All three of us have a lifetime hunting license for the state of Michigan. At the time of this story, my boy Bob was still going to college, but married.

We both had applied for a bear permit and were lucky enough to get one. My boy made plans to get up for a couple days around a weekend he could get off to try for a bear. He had never gotten one. A friend of ours helped us with the setting up of our blinds and baiting for the bear. It is not as easy as you may think. A lot of things have to fall in place for you to come out a winner. The bear were hitting a few baits, and we were hoping for a good hunt.

Bob made it home with his wife and spent the first couple of days sitting in a blind in an area where the bear had been working. All the signs looked real good, but the bear were just not moving like they should have been. If you are not in the right spot at the right time, you will strike out, and there is nothing you can do about it.

Now, as I said, Bob had sat without seeing anything the first couple of nights. He was beginning to wonder because bear permits are hard to get. He did not know the next time everything would work out for him to try for a bear. We went out to check the baits one morning when our hunting buddies had to work. We covered a number of them, and we had a plan. Back the year Bob was born, his mom had canned some plums. There were still a number of these jars down in the basement, and we figured why not and took some. As we checked one bait, we saw a big bear track in the sand. It really got our hearts pumping knowing there was a bear working. When we got back to my buddies' house, they had returned from work, and we told them about the big bear track we had spotted. There was only one problem.

You see, this nice bear track we had found was at Cliff's blind, and he also had a bear permit. Now, you know how hunting is, and ethics say that you do not hunt another person's blind. You wouldn't want them to move into yours. Besides, it would really be wrong to do simply because you saw some sign at his and not yours. But, Cliff had shot a good number of bear through the years, and he knew my boy had never gotten the chance. Cliff told him, "Bob, go sit in my blind and try your luck there." Bob went out, and we monkeyed around the house and went in to eat.

As we were sitting at the table (in Cliff's house) eating supper, we heard a three-wheeler running. We walked outside and heard it coming from the direction Bob was off hunting in. It was too early to come in without a reason, so just maybe. You know that feeling only a dad gets hoping. Bob pulled into the yard as Cliff said, "Well, what did you get?" "I don't know how big it is. It sure looked big at first, but now I don't know." Bob called my house, so his mom and wife could head out as we went back after his bear.

We got back into the area of the blind and found a really nice bear of around 300 pounds lying there. We about beat the fire out of Bob giving him a hard time about his bear. You would have to be a part of it to know what we mean. My boy, my friends-how could a person live without them? We dressed the bear out and about killed ourselves dragging it out. Just after we got it back to the house, his wife and mom pulled up, and they were as happy for him as could be. Hunting is a family time; it builds feelings within a family that money could never buy. My wife and daughter-in-law do not hunt, but they are a part of it since they know their men enjoy it.

Please take the time to picture this. Here is a friend of mine that has a chance to get a nice bear. Here is MY boy who has never

94

gotten one. My friend, and his friend, says, "Bob, go sit in my blind and try for mine." Then when MY boy, his friend, gets his bear, he is as happy as can be. It did not matter that he never got one that season or since. It was just that special feeling that true hunting friends have for each other. I thank Cliff from the bottom of Bob's dad's heart for making his first bear hunt special.

A Buddy Could Get You Killed

This is another one of those stories about bow hunters. They can be strange. I should have known something was worth watching about this guy when I first saw him on this day. I went out to my buddies' house, and this "Troll" was up to do some bow hunting. Now, up in this area if you want to practice with a bow to hunt from a tree, a lot of people just go up on their roof and shoot to simulate shooting from their tree stand. On this morning there were two or three inches of fresh snow, but the sun was now out. Our "Troll" had been up on the roof to practice, and he made a couple of shots, set his bow down up on the roof and climbed down to retrieve his arrows. Only one problem. Sitting right behind the target he had shot at were a pile of frozen sugar beets, and his arrows were stuck right in them. It took him a while to carve his arrows out of the sugar beets. All this time the sun was shining. He finally got them out and climbed up on the ladder to take a few more shots, remember, his bow was already up on the roof. As he climbed onto the roof, he found out the sun had warmed it up just enough to make it like ice under the couple of inches of snow. He would climb about half way up to his bow and slide right back down to the ladder. He could not get back up on the roof to get his bow. It was about like watching a funny home video. Finally, he got his bow and came down.

As we were standing there talking he told me (this man has bow hunted all over the country and is really good) he only hunts scrapes. He told me how he did it, and little did I know what I was in for.

That evening I was in my blind and ended up taking a little walk across a beaver pond onto an island. Here I found a good number of deer scrapes and a real good runway. Opening day of deer season was the next morning, so I sat in my blind and watched a couple of deer moving around. About 11:00 I was tired of sitting and decided to cross back over the beaver pond and see how the scrapes looked. I hit the island and walked up under the hemlocks looking down at the runway. All of a sudden, I heard something and looked up! Coming right at me, wide open, (I'm standing right in the middle of the runway) is a big deer. I try to find the safety on my rifle that I have been using since high school without any luck! At the last minute this deer turns and tears by on my right side bald as can be.

I turn around still shaking and here comes another big deer tearing right towards me! Man! There is no way I can get my gun up in time, but at least I found the safety, so if it has antlers I plan on "John Wayneing" it as it goes by. It goes by within five feet of me as bald as can be. Haaaa! my heart is going a hundred miles an hour as I look up and here comes the third deer. I drop down on my knee and drop the deer right in its tracks before it can run me over and kill me. Oh, it did have antlers. Remember, a "Troll" could get you killed. But, the fun has only started. I dress the deer out and about that time I hear my boy calling from back at the trailer.

I walk out and meet him and tell him about my adventures. We have one little problem. Remember, I was telling you I had walked across to an island. My buck was still on it. The boy did not have any boots, but I was kind enough to lend him a pair of mine, sized 13+; he wears size 9. We went through the tag alders back to the island. We cut a pole and ran it through the deer's legs and tied it to the pole. You see this all the time on those videos and it looks easy. Off we go the couple of hundred feet to the edge of the marsh. Then, the fun begins. Trip, stumble, fall, laugh, crash, what a mess! As you try to carry this buck, its head swings back and forth and throws you all off balance. What a joke those videos are!! Besides, my boy has to take two steps for each one his (mine) size 13+ boots move. By the time we got to the other side of the beaver dam, I had blood blisters on my shoulders from the pole the deer was hanging on, my back was broke in at least three places, I was sweating so bad steam was rolling off me, and we had laughed so hard my throat was sore. But, boy, did we have fun.

Just watch out for those pointers from those "Trolls". They could get you in deep trouble.

A Hunting Note: I get a kick out of people that are scared of bear. In all the years I have spent in the woods, I can count on one hand all the bear I have seen. You flat very seldom see a bear as you poke around in the woods. As kids, we used to have them come into the corner of the clearing by our hunting camp all the time. Dad would call us over and say, "Watch, there's a bear and her cubs over in the corner now. You kids stay in the yard till they leave." I did not know you were supposed to be scared of bear till I started working for the state and all those people started calling me when they saw a bear.

Besides, if you have ever hunted bear, you know they never make a noise when going through the woods unless they want to. They move just like a shadow. A three or four hundred pound bear is as quiet as can be. You will be sitting in your blind and all of a sudden look up and there they are. You never heard a thing! In fact, you can watch them move through the woods and never hear them unless they roll over a log or something.

I have come up with this "Yooper" Philosophy: There is no use wasting your time worrying about a bear getting you. They move through the woods without ever making a sound. This means, if they want you, they will have you before you even know they are there. So, why worry about something that if it wants you, it's got you!!

Northern Pike, taken from Indian Lake

Chapter 18

Conservation Officer's Stories
Upper Michigan Tales from a Game Warden's Perspective

Family Folklore

I guess there is nothing better to keep a family together than good memories of years past in family stories that are passed down. Here are a couple of tales about how things used to be.

I Was Someone Special

Well, I sure wish all the youth of today could have lived back in the "good old days" in the 40's. This is when I grew up and really got to do things with my dad. Now, before we get into the story, let me remind you that school always came first. You had better behave and do your schoolwork, and if you did, there were rewards.

Come the fall of the year, Dad would take us kids up the Norwich Road to the relative's farm. Here Dad parked his hunting "Bug". We would pump up the tires, and put gas in it. Dad would crank it to start it, and then it was off through the woods and down the old skidding trails till he hit the old railroad grade called "The Main Line." Off down The Main Line through the old potato fields till we came to the old falling down shack called Camp 3. Take a left here and off through the woods on a rough old trail with mud holes you would not believe. Finally, after maybe getting stuck a couple of times, we would come to Mill Creek where our old hunting shack was.

Our hunting "Bug" was an old Ford Model A that could sit all year. The tires would lose their air and have to be pumped up each fall. Remember, they had tubes back in those days. Check the oil; add gas, and it never in all the years I was around failed to start. They were quite the vehicles. In my first book, "A Deer Gets Revenge", there is a picture of us kids and dad sitting in our "Bug" out in front of the shack talked about in this tale.

Here on the bank of Mill Creek was a shack made of paper! The heavy construction paper that the mill in Ontonagon produced at that time. The shack had a 2x2 frame, and a roof with slates and tar paper on top. Each fall we would have to go into the shack a couple of weeks before it was to be used for deer season and fix it up. You see, because it was made out of paper, if a bear wanted to walk in and look around for something to eat, he just walked in through the walls. Then, when the bear decided to leave, he never bothered to walk back out through the same hole. On top of this, the porkies would have a field day chewing away on anything and everything that was chewable. We would remove the lath, cut pieces of paper and patch up all the holes.

Then it would be time to cut firewood for the upcoming hunting season. (This was before anyone we knew had a chain saw.) Out would come the two-man crosscut saw. I wanted to run and hide, for I knew who was going to end up on one end. I can sit here over forty years later still hearing my dad say, "Son, you just have to pull a crosscut saw your way, don't keep trying to push it back that's why it buckles. You pull your way, then I'll pull mine." You soon found out it worked great if both people did what they were supposed to. But, you would get daydreaming, push, bind up the saw and get corrected again. But, we always got the wood cut.

After that, it was off down the hill to the creek to clean out the water hole where we got all our cooking and drinking water during deer season. Patch up the outhouse, and our work was done.

Come a couple of days before hunting season, and it was time to haul the gear back into deer camp. We would usually do it with the "Bug". But, if the weather that fall had been really bad, the road and mud holes would be more than the "Bug" could handle. You would have to know what Ontonagon red clay is to know what I am talking about. You have never really ever been stuck in your life unless you got stuck in this type clay. If it were too bad for the "Bug", we would take a team of horses using a jumper. (A jumper is two logs with some boards between them that you stand on. There is a chain through the front of the logs that comes up to hook on the whippletree, so the team can pull it.) This never did get stuck for some reason.

We would take in a radio that was battery operated. It had about a zillion (a boy's count) flashlight batteries hooked together in a big package that weighed about a ton. This huge battery would last just about the two weeks of deer season, and then it was history. (I still have this radio today.) We would haul in the old lamps and

100

other equipment to get ready for Dad's brother, cousin, and some friends to come up from "down state."

I lived for Friday the first week of deer season because I knew that on Friday Dad would come to town from camp. Now understand, back in those days this was not an easy project. But, he never failed to come get me! I even got to miss a day of school if my marks had been good. It was off to deer camp with Dad. At first it was Dad with his rifle and me with my trusty Red Ryder BB gun out to help Dad get a deer. Never dreaming it wasn't a real gun. You would finally get back to camp, and it was great. You have to remember that back in those days a boy never saw a whole lot of treats. But, deer camp was different! My uncle would bring all kinds of great things up from down-state, from apples, to candy bars of all kinds, to always a keg of good apple cider. A boy had it made.

We cooked in camp on an old wood cook stove that sat in one corner. The fridge was a wooden box (like one things were shipped in back then) nailed to a tree. The gun racks and places to hang your clothes were all whittled from forks from trees. At night all there was for light was lantern light. But, I guess the best part was when it came time to go to bed. You see, back then you slept on what was called a "tick". Mom would take a number of flour sacks and sew them all together making a big outfit that looked like an overgrown pillowcase. Then you would take these into camp along with a number of bails of straw. You would take the straw and fill up the case Mom had made making what was called a "straw tick". This is what you slept on. It was neat! You would crawl up there and sink down about a foot; Dad and usually one other of the party were on each side of you. You then covered with about a dozen homemade quilts to keep warm because usually the fire went out, or just about, at night. Man! This was a great way to live for a "Yooper" kid.

This was just a great time to be growing up. Come morning, the first brave soul from the lower bunk would crawl out and build a fire. Then, jump back in bed till it started to produce a little heat and warm the shack up. The older hunters would get out of bed to start to get things in gear for the day, while I stayed up in the warm upper bunk and watched all the action while still under the warm covers. When breakfast was ready, I would get dressed while still under the covers. This was a true art back in those days.

Then, it was out of bed for breakfast. Each and every member of the shack crew had a job they had to do. My uncle always did the cooking, others would pick up, and others were to clean up after the meals. Remember that doing kitchen type work at deer camp is not sissy type work at all.

After things were picked up, it was time to make plans for the day's hunt and off we would go. I can remember those times up at camp with Dad just like it happened this past deer season, and it was over forty years ago. Why? Because at those times I was someone special; I was Dad's hunting buddy, and you could not ask for a better deal.

My Grandpa

My Grandpa Theiler was a guy you all should have known. A young boy could never tell when Grandpa was telling a tale where the truth ended and his story began. It sure was an interesting time being around him. Now, Grandpa grew up on a farm near Tomahawk, WI. In his family, there were thirteen boys and each one had a sister, as Grandpa always said. Their mother could have run this country with the system she had set up on the farm to keep control of things. Grandpa used to always tell us kids, "The only time we ever went to school was when things were all caught up on the farm. Then we could only go in warm weather because we didn't own any shoes. In the summer during the warm weather, there was not any school, so we really didn't go too often."

The thing that always amazed me was the successful people that came out of this system. There were lawyers, doctors, businessmen, schoolteachers, etc. Now we have our modern way of doing things in school, and we turn out kids that can't read and write. We missed something somewhere. My Grandpa could sit and watch TV back when they had all these question and answer type shows on and answer 90% of the questions asked! And he never went to school, except when he got a chance.

When we would go down to Tomahawk to a wedding or something, everybody wanted to stay at Uncle George's. He was one of the best storytellers of them all. Uncle George was a vet, so he got to come across a lot of tales he could try out on us kids. Besides, there was a bakery right across the alley from his house, so when he fixed breakfast, it was a treat from the bakery. I heard this story about Uncle George a number of times. In fact, when he was getting up in years, there was a story about this in the Milwaukee, WI. paper.

It seemed that Uncle George was working on the farm one day and decided he would like to be a veterinarian. So, he packed his bags and went off to the Chicago area to attend vet school. He worked his way along and made it to the end of his senior year at veterinarian school. In fact, he was due to be honored as one of the top students in his graduating class.

Time came for setting things up for graduation, so the head of the school called Uncle George into his office. Uncle George sat down, and the Dean said, "George, you are due to graduate as one of the top students in this year's class, but we noticed we do not have a copy of your high school diploma in your files. Could you get us a copy?" Uncle George looked at him and said, "I don't have one." He was asked, "What do you mean, you don't have one?" "I don't have one. I never went to high school!" "What do you mean you never went to high school? How can you then be here in our college if you never finished high school?" Uncle George replied, "I was on the farm one day, and I always wanted to be a veterinarian. So, I just packed my bags and came down and enrolled. Nobody ever asked me if I had a high school diploma till today."

The Dean did not really know what to say except, "You are not supposed to be here if you never finished high school, and here you are at the top of this year's graduating class. I'll get back to you."

The way the story is told, the head of the school called a meeting of the board, and they tried to figure out what to do about this farm boy from Northern Wisconsin. They finally decided that seeing he had passed everything with flying colors and was to graduate with honors, they would make an exception to the rules and give him his diploma.

The newspaper stated that as far as they know he is the only person to ever graduate from this college who had not finished high school.

IS the story all true the way Grandpa used to tell it? We did not really care or even think about it because Grandpa was about the best storyteller in the whole world.

Chapter 19

Conservation Officer's Stories
Upper Michigan Tales from a Game Warden's Perspective

More Snowmobiling

In this neck of the woods during the long winter months, the main way to get back in and check fishermen on the many inland lakes is by snowmachine. As I have stated before, I have put thousands and thousands of miles on my issued snowmachines. It made for some interesting trips. Here are a few of the highlights just to let you know what can happen.

Open It Up!

One day, we were working up in the National Forest checking some lakes. In this area there were a number of registered trout lakes that were closed to fishing during the winter. For this reason, there were always those that had to try them out. On this day, we had checked a few lakes and decided to head back into these other two lakes and check them out.

Now remember, when you hit these lakes on a snowmachine, you wind it up to see if there are any fishermen and get to them before they can pull their lines. We hit this one lake called Ironjaw coming in through the woods. I had never been on this lake before, so I opened it up and headed down to the far end and around a bend to see if there were any fishermen there. I came around the bend doing about fifty miles an hour and straightened it out. It was only a small bay off this end and the woods were just a short ways off. But, as I looked up, I saw nothing but open water about ten feet in front of me up to the woods! I knew on the bare ice I could never stop. I would just lock up the track and slide on the ice into the open water in front of me. All I thought to do was squeeze the gas and get going as fast as I could and try to go across the water into the woods. The water was an area where there is muck almost to the surface, and the water in this type area freezes last. I opened it up as I yelled at my buddy to stop, and off across the water I went! I made it to the woods into the trees with mud and water flying all over the place, but I was safe on solid ground.

But, I Didn't See That

This day I was working out on Indian Lake. Now you have to remember that Indian Lake is miles and miles long. You get fishermen that take ice-fishing shanties out on the lake and leave them there all winter. The first of the year when the ice forms, there is little or no snow, but as the winter goes along, the snow comes and piles up on the lake. When the winds blow, the snow drifts off across the lake. This makes for some interesting trips. When you have ice fishing shanties sitting out there, the wind blows around them, and the snow drifts off the backside. The problem is when it is sunny and you are running across the lake, there is not any depth perception with everything being a sun-glaring white.

As I stated before, you would hit the lake and have to open the snowmachine up to try and get up to the fishermen before they could get rid of their extra lines or illegal fish. You would hit the lake; open it up and everything would be going fine. That is until you came to an area behind an ice-fishing shanty where the snow had drifted up three to four feet. The next thing you knew you were airborne trying to do a handstand on a snowmachine at fifty or sixty miles an hour. It is not a nice feeling. I never lost my snowmachine, but I took some jarring landings-always landing back on the seat. Then, I would kind of look around to see if any of the fishermen out there saw this brilliant move I had just made. Hopefully not.

Compass Shot

On another day, I was out on Indian Lake, and the wind came up. All of a sudden, I could not see a thing; there was a complete whiteout. I stopped the snowmachine on the downwind side of an ice fishing shanty. I had to try and figure out what to do. There are only a couple of problems running a snowmachine out on Indian Lake. It is called Big Springs and the Cope Bridge. In both these areas there is open water almost all winter long. I did not want to head in either of these two directions. So, I took out my compass and took a reading. I figured that from where I was if I went straight east I would hit the shore over by Dawson Road.

I took my compass bearing, started up the snow machine, held the skis right straight and headed out. I did not travel too fast wanting to make sure I kept the handlebars and skis straight east where I had taken the compass shot. I must have run five or ten minutes and should be nearing the shore. All of a sudden, I could not believe it! I came right back to the ice fishing shanty I had left ten minutes ago! I knew it was the same one by the wood it was made out of.

This time I got my compass out, took a compass shot, ran a little ways, took another compass shot, ran a little farther, and on and on till I hit the shore on the east side of the lake.

The U.P.
Upper Michigan

Lake Superior

Ontonagon

Area I Worked
District IV
Area 7

Canada

Wisconsin

Escanaba

Manistique

Lake Huron

Lake Michigan

300 miles north of Milwaukee

300 Miles from Manistique to Lansing

Northern
Michigan

Down State

Lansing(capital)

First work
station

Chapter 20

Conservation Officer's Stories
Upper Michigan Tales from a Game Warden's Perspective

An Old Man's Dream

This is a short story about how the Lord blessed in the sale of my books that appeared in a number of newspapers and magazines. In my travels, I get asked all the time how things are going, so I put this together.

From 0 to 20,000 in one year

Synopses of My Book Selling Adventures: by John A. Walker

I guess everyone has a dream or two as they go along in life. One of mine is to leave a scholarship fund for young people from the church I attend with my family, Bethel Baptist Church in Manistique, MI, where I have been in charge of the youth program for almost twenty years.

When I retired as a Michigan Conservation Officer in June of 1991, I placed $3,000 in a scholarship fund at Bethel Baptist Church to get things started. Being a realist, I knew that $3,000 would not be enough for the fund to carry on year after year, so I began to think.

For the last six or seven years that I worked as a Game Warden, I wrote a weekly article for a weekly local newspaper. In this article, "The Fish Report", I would tell stories about working as a Michigan Conservation Officer and tales about growing up in Michigan's Upper Peninsula. People really liked these Backwoods Tales with their humor, and a number of people encouraged me to put some of these stories into a book.

From these newspaper articles, my first book, "A Deer Gets Revenge", came out in the fall of 1993. Here I sat in my garage with 5,000 books written by a person nobody ever heard of except the readers of the Manistique-Pioneer Tribune. There was only one thing to do I placed some boxes of books in my car and started off into the book selling business. I went to "Mom and Pop's corner store" and asked if they would like to sell a few books for me. I stopped at gas stations and restaurants and asked them if they would like to sell some books. I went to sporting goods stores and grocery stores and asked them if they would like to help me out. All this without the faintest idea what I was doing or how it would work out. But, I had 5,000 books to sell to someone and needed all the help I could get. I sure met a lot of people. I went to radio stations and asked, "If I give you a couple of books, would you mention my book on your station?" I wrote outdoor writers and national sporting good chains and asked them if they would help me with my book.

During this time I would sell books one at a time and sell books hundreds at a time to big bookstores. My big break came when a local party that has his own outdoor show on TV-6 here in the U.P. called and offered to help me out (Buck LeVasseur, "Discovering Program"). It started the ball rolling.

Later I was standing in a radio station talking to Ken (Disc-jockey), when a party that has a radio talk show mentioned that his guest for the day had cancelled. Ken talked to him about me and the book I had written. The host came out and said, "If you are willing to wing it, we'll go for it." What did I have to lose?!

A week or so later I was up in my hometown and stopped to talk to a lady who had her own radio program for years. She was on the air as I stopped by, so she just said, "Come on in." Then, we talked about my book on her program.

Things like this happened that I had no control over. They were always happening. Doors were opened and opportunities given that money could not buy. I could never repay these people who helped me out.

Later on I would be standing in a big bookstore waiting to ask the manager if they would like to try and sell my book. As I stood there a person would walk up and ask, "Where did you buy that book?" I would say, "I didn't buy it. I wrote it." They would ask, "Do they sell it here?" The manager said, "Hopefully, in just a minute." I would sell four to five books while they were filling out the paperwork to sell my book in their store. This happened a number of times.

Then another outdoor writer (a real one from Marquette, MI.) mentioned my book in his outdoor column. A newspaper outdoor writer from Green Bay, WI, told about my book in his outdoor article, and local newspapers around the state wrote articles about my book. God blessed.

Bass Pro Shop out of Springfield, MO, sold my book in one of their catalogs, Jay's Sporting Goods in Clare, MI, (a big outdoor store) sold some of my books, and Bronner's Christmas Wonderland (one of Michigan's biggest tourist attractions) ordered and sold my books. The list goes on and on. What a year it has been!

I was asked to attend a number of outdoor shows by a local marine dealer to sell my books and meet people in his display area. I met so many people that liked my first book at these shows that in June 1994 my second book titled "A Bucket of Bones" came out.

Again, it was off to the races with my bookmobile. The first year my two books were out I had over 20,000 books published.

People always ask me if I made any money off my books? I answer, "I'm not quite sure! But, the scholarship fund now has over 10,000 dollars in it. ($1.00 from each book sold goes into this fund.) The IRS was better off in '93 than it was the year before and should be better off in '94 than in '93."

I guess the best part of the whole thing is the six scholarships we have given out in the past year to help young people go to college. One we gave out was to a girl washing dishes at a Big Boy Restaurant who had a dream.

This lady's dream was to someday go off to college to be a secretary, but now she was in her 30's. When I heard this, I told her one night at church, "Wendy, put in for the scholarship to help out. "She told me she didn't know if she could seeing she was out of school for so long. She applied, and one Sunday night I got a call asking me if my wife and I could give her a ride down to a college by Milwaukee, WI, to let her go after her dream. We did, and she is there now trying to catch her dream. It sure made the wife and I feel great just to play a little part.

In closing, I guess the most interesting thing about writing these two books is all the letters I have received from people that have read them. I tell people that women are my best salespeople because they seem to love the books. Why? I cannot say; it just turned out that way through no skill of mine. There have been letters from state college presidents, corporation presidents, school principals, and people of all ages and walks of life. It seems that the way I tell stories with my backwoods grammar, people can kick off their shoes, relax, and enjoy reading without a backwoods tale taxing their brain at all.

I guess after a hard day that would be good for all of us.

Backwoods Glossary

Up here in the Great North Woods, there is a tendency to use terms or phrases to make a point. To some of you, they may be used in a way you never realized they could be. Other words or terms, you may just have not had the opportunity to ever use. This Backwoods Glossary is to help you out in understanding why we talk like we do.

U.P. (Upper Michigan): If, for some strange reason, you have never traveled in Michigan, these two letters would seem strange to you. First, understand that Michigan has two peninsulas the upper and lower. The Lower Peninsula is made up of two parts, Lower Michigan and Northern Michigan. But, the really important part of Michigan lies across the Mackinaw Bridge. This part of Michigan is called the U.P., for the Upper Peninsula of Michigan. The people up here in the U.P. live in their own little world and like it that way. The only problem is that most of the laws are passed down in Lower Michigan to correct their problems, and then they affect us, who may not even be part of that problem. Some of the Big City folks that pass these laws never have learned to understand and love the U.P. like we that live here do. The natives of the U.P. have trouble understanding the "why-for" about some of these laws; therefore they feel they really must not apply to them.

Two of the biggest industries in the U.P. are paper mills and the men that work in the woods supplying trees to these mills so they can produce their product. There are probably more colleges in the U.P., per capita, than anywhere else in the country. But even with this, there are still a lot of natives up here that feel you could sure ruin a good person if you sent them to one of these colleges. News of a serious crime will travel from one side of the U.P. to the other like a wild fire. Because most people up here are not used to it. To them, serious crimes are when someone takes a deer or some fish illegally and is dumb enough to get caught. They don't even take these crimes to seriously unless the poacher should step over the line and get to greedy.

Sports teams that play teams from other towns in the U.P. always seem to have relatives, or friends, on the other team. Everyone knows someone, or someone that married someone, that knew someone from over there. To win a state championship, you have to beat those teams from "down state". To do this is a dream come true for any red-blooded U.P. boy or girl.

When I was growing up, we had only had part-time radios. So we had to be Green Bay (Wisconsin) Packer and Milwaukee Brave fans. As a boy living in the Western U.P., we could not pick up any radio stations that carried broadcast of the teams from Lower Michigan. For this reason, we grew up feeling that we were a state unto ourselves. We could not be part of Lower Michigan, because it was just to far away, and the only way to get there was by boat. We knew we were not part of Wisconsin, so we were just the Good Old U.P.

Up here in the U.P., where life is tough, but things are good, and it is just a great place to live.

Some backwoods (U.P.) terms:

2-TRACK:(roads) The U.P. has hundreds of miles of this type of roads. All these roads consist of are two tire ruts worn into the ground from all the vehicle travel throughout the years. Usually you have a high, grass-covered center and mud holes in the low spots. This is one of the reasons that so many people in the U.P. feel you cannot live without a 4x4 pickup. These roads are never worked on or improved and you get what you see.

Blacktop Roads: These are the 2-tracks, which are worse than unimproved roads. They are covered by mud or clay and it is a real trick to stay between the trees on some of these. There are also a lot of these type roads for which the U.P. is famous. Many a fishermen or hunter has spent hours and hours trying to get out of one of these blacktop roads, usually after you misjudged what you were getting into. Two of the first things I learned after becoming a Game Warden stationed in the U.P. were: It's hard to get 2-ton stuck at fifty miles an hour, so wind it up and keep moving. The other one follows point one, you are never really stuck till you stop. In other words, if one of these blacktop areas sneaks up on you, floor it and don't stop 'til you reach high ground or hit something unmovable.

Poachers: These are not people that cook eggs in hot water, but may get themselves in hot water now and then. They are outlaws that rob the honest hunters and fishermen of their chance to get game and fish legally. In years past, it was a way of life in the U.P. that was passed down from generation to generation. When it was an accepted thing to do, the Game Warden not only had a hard time catching the poachers, but he usually had an even harder time trying to get a conviction in the local courts.

Shining: (Shinning, Shining, Shiners), Shiners are the poachers that use a spotlight to look for deer at night, in order to shoot them. Until the fines got to high, it was the way that a lot of the outlaws did their hunting here in the U.P. They would take a pair of spotlights, hook them up in their vehicle, and then drive around while casting the rays of the spotlights out into fields or an old orchard, until they spotted a deer. The deer, blinded by the bright light, would stand there staring at the light while the poacher got out his gun and shot it. There is really no sport in it, because it is so deadly. You will notice I spelled shinning, with two "n's" at times. Well, I did this on my tickets for dozens of cases throughout the years; until a State Trooper told me it was spelled wrong. He said it should only have one "n", so on the next couple tickets I changed how I spelled shining. You see for years, when I caught someone hunting deer at night with a spotlight, the only thing I would write for a charge on the ticket was the one word "shinning". With the one word spelled, Shinning, they knew what they did, I knew what they had done, and most important the average U.P. Judge knew what they were standing before him for doing. Well, the first time I caught a crew out spotlighting for deer and put shining (with one n) on their ticket they pled "Not Guilty". The spelling must have confused them and so was I.

Spearers: These are people that have a way of taking fish with the use of a spear. The spear can have from three to five prongs, with pointed tips; these prongs have barbs on the end to hold the fish on the spear after they spear it. Now in some areas, it is legal to spear certain types of non-game fish. The problem the Game Warden has is with those that spear trout, salmon, walleye, etc. or "game fish". When these fish come into real shallow water to spawn, a Game Warden will spend hour after hour watching the fish spawning in these areas.

Extractors: This is a term for those illegal fishermen that may come along a creek with a spear trying to extract the spawning fish from the creek. They may use other devices besides a spear. For instance, a weighted hook, hand nets, their hands, etc.

Gill Netters: These are people, both legal and illegal, that use a gill net to take fish. In some areas, there is a commercial fishery allowed with the use of gill nets, but in Michigan it is never legal for "sport" fishermen to use a gill net to take fish. A gill net is made up of nylon string in little squares (it looks something like a small woven wire fence) built so the fish will swim into the net putting their head through the square openings. Then, they get caught when their larger body will not fit through the squares and their gills keep them from backing out of the nets. I have observed illegal gill net fishermen take hundreds of pounds of steelhead in a couple of hours, if they set their gill nets in the right spot.

Fish house or fish shed: In areas of the U.P., along the great lakes where there is a legal commercial fishery, most of those businesses involved have a building where they clean, box in ice, and store their catch. They may also repair their nets in this building. On account of the smell around a full time commercial fishing operation, most of these sheds are located away from any residence. They also may be on the riverbank where the commercial fisherman ties up his fish tug. For this reason they are often used for illegal activity, sometimes by others than those that own them.

Deer camp: A deer camp can be any type of building used for offering protection from the elements. It is also used as a "get-a-way from home during the hunting season. Some are as nice as any house, better than some, while others may be made out of plastic, heavy paper, scrap lumber, or anything to keep the weather out. The following rules are some of the usual type that are proper for deer camp life.

(1) You cannot shave or take a bath, no matter how many days you may be staying at camp. You are allowed to wash your face and hands. But this is your own choice; you do not have to if you do not want to. This is one reason young boys love to go to deer camp with Dad.

(2) There is no proper way to dress while at deer camp, if it feels good wear it! You can even wear the same clothes all week long. This includes your socks, if you can catch them after the first three days at camp.

(3) The "menu" is always made up of all the "proper" things that you cannot afford to eat all the rest of the year at home. Both good and bad for you.

(4) It is never wrong to tell a "true" story on another camp member. Remembering it is of more value if you can dress it up a little to make him suffer all the time you are telling it. During the telling of his misfortune we must all remember that we will all pay for our mistakes, sooner or later, if and when our hunting "buddies" find out about them.

(5) It is a crime, punishable by banishment, to talk about school, or schoolwork, or any work for that matter while at deer camp.

(6) You can throw, hang or just leave your socks and clothes anywhere they land when you remove them. You can hang your wet socks on anything that has something to hang them from to try and dry them out before the next days hunt. Always remembering it is "most" important to have dry socks by daybreak the next morning.

(7) What may be called work at home is not work at deer camp. Therefore getting things done at deer camp is not classified as work, but a team effort. For this reason, it is not wrong for a boy to do dishes, sweep a floor, pick up trash (that he missed getting in the trash can when he threw it that way, with one of his famous hook shots), or even do what Dad asks him to do, the first time Dad asks him to do it.

You would have to spend a week at a real U.P. deer camp to really know the true feeling of being a U.P. deer hunter. With these easy-to-apply rules, you can see why deer camp life is so important to a boy during his informative teenage years. It is really important that a young man start out with a proper perspective on life.

Big House: This is the Michigan State Capital; from some areas of the U.P. it can be over 400 miles away. In Lansing, this is where "they" compile all the rules and ideas that are put out to confuse the average hunter or fisherman, while out in the field. It is the feeling of a lot of U.P. sportsmen, that most of those that work down there, in Lansing's Big House, never in their lives set foot in the real out-of-doors, or wet a fishing line in a back woods stream. What they know, they got from someone that wrote a book without ever having set their feet in a real woods, or having gone backwoods fishing either. It is just passed on from desk to desk, year after year, put into volumes of rules and law books that we out in the field have to learn to live with. This while trying to enjoy ourselves out in the real Northwood's, Michigan's U.P.

Wifee: (W-IF-EE; wify) this is one's wife. To pronounce it right, you say the "W" sound, then the "IF", than draw out the "EE".

Big Lake: This can be any of the Great Lakes that border Michigan. Instead of saying, " I went fishing out on Lake Michigan Saturday". A native from the U.P. would say, "I went fishing on the Big Lake Saturday afternoon".

Off-road vehicles: ATV'S, ORV'S, dirt bikes, etc. These may be any of the type vehicles that are made primarily to operate off an improved road. Some may be homemade, while dealers sell others. In the U.P. you will find a lot of these used by sportsmen to get around when hunting and fishing.

Game Wardens: Conservation Officer, C.O.'s, and Game Wardens are all one and the same, up here in the U.P. They have been around for better than 100 years serving the people of Michigan. The stories they can tell and those told on them are told over and over around the U.P. This is how my newspaper, story telling got started.

Holiday Stations: Holiday? Here, in Michigan's U.P., you always hear the expression, "I'm going to stop by Holiday on the way". Some of you folks may not understand what a Holiday is and how far advanced the U.P. is over other areas of our country. I'll try to explain. Holiday; here in the North Country is a gas station-store. The Holiday Stations have been around for years and years, and in the U.P. they are like a mini-mall. The U.P. and Holiday were way ahead of the rest of the world on this idea of doing all your shopping in one stop. Get your gas plus whatever else you may need here at the Holiday. Sometimes it just takes awhile for you all to catch up to us, Yoopers.

Years ago when Christmas time came around, you went down to the Holiday. Here you did all your Christmas shopping. It had a great toy selection, in fact, in most U.P. towns the best to be found. If company dropped in for a surprise visit and you needed food items, off you went to the Holiday to get what you needed. When hunting and fishing season rolled around, they put out a paper and sales ad to get you into the Holiday to fill your needs, everything from guns and ammo, to poles, hooks, and line. If you snagged your waders, off you went to the Holiday for new ones. If your feet got cold out deer hunting, off to the Holiday for warm footgear you went. If your motorized deer blind broke down on a weekend, off to the auto parts section of the Holiday to get what you needed. What am I saying? Before the rest of the world was smart enough to think about putting other than gas and oil supplies in their gas stations the Holiday was there. Now they have moved up one more step because most Holiday Stations have copies of my books for sale.

Remember when traveling through the U.P., if a town does not have a Holiday station, keep on trucking till you find one because that town you are in has not arrived yet!

Copper Country: In so many parts of my book, you will read about things that took place in the Copper Country. This area covers what is called the Keweenaw Peninsula over to the area of the copper mines to the west. Those of us that lived in the Copper Country felt you were going into the world of the great unknown if you left Ontonagon, Houghton, Baraga, or Keweenaw County. In fact, a person growing up when I did may have left the Copper Country for the first time when he went into the service. The Copper Country is really a melting pot of people from all over the world. When I was growing up, it was nothing for some of the old folks not being able to speak English; they talked in their native language. In fact, one of the things that really bugged a teenage boy from the Copper Country was when there were a couple of girls your buddy and you wanted to get to know, and they would talk back and forth in Finnish, and we did not have the foggiest idea what they were saying. The history of the Copper Country is both interesting and unreal if you study it. A person could move away and be gone for years, but when asked where they are from, they always answer the Copper Country.

In the Copper Country, everybody knows somebody that knows somebody else. When on a radio show talking about my first book, "*A Deer Gets Revenge*", a party called in and wanted to know if I was Harry Theiler's grandson. Then another party called in and wanted to know if I was Tim Walker's brother. (Tim is my brother that lives in a home in Hancock, MI, in the Copper Country). Copper Country people are special people that help make up a place called the U.P. where people know and care about each other. Come visit the U.P. and Copper Country someday, and you will see what I mean.

The other day: I keep telling my kids and the readers of my newspaper article that when I use the saying, "The other day", it could mean anytime between birth and death. It is up to the person you are talking too, to try and figure out what era you are talking about. Up here in the U.P., a party could start to tell you a hunting story by saying, " *The other day a buddy and I....*" and the story may have taken place back in the forties. (1940's) You have to remember that good stories never really get old; they just get better and added to in the telling of them. There was one officer I worked with could he tell stories! He would get going into a story and you would sit there and listen. Pretty soon bits and pieces would start to ring a bell. Then all of a sudden it would dawn on you that you were with him when "his story" took place, but you really never remembered it happening like he was telling it, or could it have? One of my boys called me from college a while back (another one of those times that means nothing in U.P. phrases) to ask me about the history of the 60's. This was for a paper he had to do for a history course. I told him, "Son, the 60's do not qualify as history yet. That is when your dad says, you know the other day, or awhile back, and that makes it today not history."

Exspurt: Sometimes in the U.P. we have our own way of spelling and understanding things. Here is one of those terms. I have a buddy that is a U.P. potato farmer. (You have to really wonder about anybody that tries to farm in the U.P.) But this buddy has a great definition for all those exspurts that rule down in the Big House. It is one of those terms you have to think about, but the more you think about it, the more you feel that this potato farmer may go down in history as a great U.P. philosopher. We will get talking about all those rules and laws the exspurts down in Lansing and Washington pass that are totally unreal, and my buddy will say, "Always remember that an ex-spurt is only a drip under pressure!" Now, I wonder.....

But then, you have all these TV shows on with an outdoor Exspurt on just about everything. Let's be real now. Do they ever get skunked out there fishing? Do you ever see them spending all day baiting hooks for the kids and getting the kids' lines untangled? Or get the boat unloaded and the motor won't start? Somehow, someway, I get the feeling these exspurts have never hunted or fished out there in the real world.

Let me give you an example of an Exspurt. One night I happened to be going through the cable channels and came across this Exspurt fisherman who had his own TV show. It happened that on this show he was fishing an area off Lake Superior that I was in charge of, so I decided to watch this show. Here is our Exspurt telling people how it should be done and where the nice steelhead fishing is in the U.P. As I watched, I couldn't believe it. So I got on the phone and called a Conservation Officer that worked for me and worked the area in the program. I told him, "John, you blew it and missed one. "He replied, "You must be watching the same program I'm watching." Then we both had a good laugh. Why? Because here was this Exspurt going along a trout stream running out of Lake Superior with an illegal device used to take trout in the spring of the year in that area! I told John, "Maybe we ought to send him a ticket in the mail. We have what he's doing on film, and he is even telling us he's doing it. "But you have to understand that this fishing Exspurt was a "troll"(a person that lives below the Big Mac Bridge.), and therefore, you get what you pay for. Now, remember what an Exspurt is, "A drip under pressure", and life will be a lot easier to understand.

Huskavarina edumacation; There has always been a feeling that there is more wisdom learned at the back end of a chain saw than you learn in college. The more some of us see and hear what is going on in our country, the more we have to wonder. It was always an amazement to those that worked out in the field for the government to see someone go off to the "Big House" on a promotion and forget everything they learned out in the field in the first six-months they were there! In fact, some of us always felt that about halfway down through the lower peninsula there was an invisible force field that made up a brain sucking machine, and by the time they passed through this going to the "Big House", they were useless to us living in the U.P.

We used to suggest that everyone after about a year or two down in Lansing's or Washington's "Big House" ought to have to spend six months back in the woods on the working end of a chain saw to get the feeling for how the real world lives again. That is why the U.P. is a special place, because from the woods, to the mines, to the papers mills, most of its people have a Husavarina Edumacation.

Sometimes I think it makes them special people as you can see by some of my stories.

Yoopers: Have you ever been asked, "What's a Yooper?" It seems that there are certain terms that the real world has not used yet. If you take the Upper Peninsula of Michigan abbreviated, namely "The U.P. and sound it out what do you get? It has to be the word Yooper. Therefore all the good people (natives only) that make their homes in the U.P. of Michigan have to be Yooper. Right?

Up here in Yooper Country we have our own jokes, our own Yooper singing groups, our own terms, and a great life style.

The one thing that you want to remember is that you are born a True Yooper. It cannot be bought, you cannot get it by living here for years and years, and you must be born a Yooper. We have a real problem with Trolls (Those that live below the Big Mac Bridge.) coming up to Yooper land then trying to act like or become one of us, it just cannot be done! You either have it or you don't. You can come see us, we are glad when you spend your money here, we like you for a friend, but remember when you leave Yooper Land you leave as you came, not as a Yooper.

The Backwoods Glossary is an ever-growing project of backwoods terms. In each new book that comes out, I include the Glossary from previous books and add a new chapter. I have to do this for those that may not have all my books. They just flat need the glossary to help them better understand the stories.

"Bugs": Back when I was a kid, it was the time before anyone knew what a 4x4 was. If a person in our neck of the woods did know what they were, they sure could never have afforded to buy one. In fact, the only 4x4 you ever heard of was a "Jeep". For this reason a hunter that wanted to get around on the old railroad grades and 2-tracks had to build his own vehicle to do it with. These home-made hunting vehicles were called "Bugs". You would be amazed at what some of the hunters and trappers came up with. Ours was an old Model A with nothing but the frame, windshield, hood, and front seats. The back was a wooden box in which to throw your shovel, chains, and other gear for when you got stuck. And you got stuck in that Ontonagon red clay!! You then put on the biggest size tires you could find that would fit to give you more clearance. After all this was done, you had a hunting "Bug".

I know one guy that could build about anything who had made one up that had chain drive back then. It was really neat to see and would go just about anywhere. You could hardly hurt these "Bugs" because there wasn't enough on them to hurt. One day my dad was coming down the Main Line railroad grade when all of a sudden smoke came pouring out from under the hood! He stopped, jumped off; flipped open the hood and flames came flying out. He grabbed his packsack and beat out the flames. Checking the "Bug" over he found where it had spilled gas, and this caught on fire. After checking it out, he got back on it, started it up and off we drove. There was really nothing to ruin on a "Bug" back then because a vehicle like this only had about a half dozen wires. A "Bug" was really neat and the first vehicle most kids like me ever drove back in those days.

Hunting: I can still hear my dad telling me, "If you ever become a meat hunter, I'll find you no matter where you are and kick your seat! Always remember that hunting is the time to get away from things and have fun with those you like to be around. If you are lucky enough to get something besides, it is just a bonus."

I have tried to live up to what my dad taught me back then because it would be too hard to walk through the woods hunting while all the time looking over my shoulder watching for dad coming up behind me. I think as you read my tales in my three books you can get my feelings about hunting. Some of the best times we have ever had we came home skunked. Now, don't think we don't like it when we are successful, but we don't build everything on just this. In fact, I am not sure we don't have more fun just before deer season as we scout around looking for deer signs and trying to outwit the deer in figuring out just how they are moving around. Sometimes you guess right, sometimes you don't.

I just wish some of these "Exspurt" hunting and fishing shows that are all on cable TV now would show more of the true side of hunting-the days you get skunked, but still had a great time with your buddies. I think the public out there would better understand hunting and the hunter if this were done.

Dad: I sure wish every boy growing up had a dad like mine. He worked hard at the paper mill, but he always had time for his family. He was not a well-educated person as we would rate education today, but he had more wisdom than almost anybody I have ever met. He was an honest man, and if he said he would do something, you better believe he would do his best to see that it got done. He loved to hunt, but it was the time spent with his boys out there that made it special. One day we were out hunting with Dad. He had to go back to town to attend a union meeting for the mill because at this time he was an officer in the union. He looked at me and said, "I guess it's time for me to resign from the union. When it keeps me away from time with my boys, it's time to give it up." He did. I never really realized till years later what a choice he had made. It was important for him to be a part of the union and to be elected as an officer by his fellow workers. He did not take it lightly. But, his family and his boys were more important even when it hurt. I just hope I have a portion of his values and that I can pass them on to my children as they grow up. I had a great dad and hope you can see it as you read some of my backwoods tales.

U.P. Learning Curve: I guess that to explain what I am trying to get across in some of my U.P. stories about how the out-of-doors can be used to train up a child to be a good citizen, I could tell this story. It's true, as you go into the main intersection in Ontonagon, you will see a little triangle. On this triangle is a little rock monument with a number of names on it. Some of these are friends that I went to school and played with growing up. These are the names of the residents of Ontonagon County who lost their lives over in Vietnam during the war. I have often sat and thought how lucky I was to be blessed with the life and family I had when theirs was snuffed out at so young an age.

As I recall it so many years later, the news kept coming home to Ontonagon that another boy had lost his life in that land so far away from the backwoods of Ontonagon. As the list grew, some people started to wonder why so high a percentage of those being

124

killed over there were from this little U.P. town of ours. As the list added a few more names, someone finally got hold of people who knew who to contact in Washington to find out what was going on. Some people did some checking, and the answer came back something like this.

"As these boys end up in the service, either by joining or the draft, they seem to have that special quality that makes them end up being trainable. They are the type youth that have pride in what they do; get along with the other service people, and the officers. They end up being where the action is because they are the type people you can depend on. When this happens, and they are where the action is, you have more of them hurt and killed."

I guess we should be proud of the type youth the U.P. turns out even when it hurts as your buddies are sent home for the last time.

Girl Hunters: There is nothing that can ruin a good hunting camp quicker then having a girl in the group! That was till both my boys were married and moved away and Dad was left with only his baby girl to go out hunting with him. Then, the rules had to change. My girl is an excellent shot and likes to go out. But, a girl will just always be a girl.

We went on a duck-hunting trip one day and were jump shooting some ponds. We came to this one where we had to walk back in. It was a warm fall day not made for walking with all your hunting gear on. Cathy went in one side of the lake, and some ducks took off; she dropped one right off. When she shot this duck, the forearm on her shotgun fell apart. The plastic piece that butts up against the metal broke in half. I stuck it back on and told her it should stay.

Some of the ducks had landed on the far side of the lake, so I went all the way around the lake to try and kick them up over her. It was hard, hot going in the water and marsh around the lake. I worked my way to the far side and could not locate the ducks. I continued around the lake to the far end, now sweating like crazy. As I came around the far end and was working my way back to Cathy, I yelled, "Cathy! Can you see the ducks? They have to be over by you!" She stepped out and yelled, "What?" (The normal question that an average teenager asks an adult no matter what they hear."

As she took a step and yelled, the ducks took off from right at her feet!! I figured they were in the blind with her. I yelled, "Shoot!!" But, she never fired a shot. I finally got around to where she was and asked her why she never shot. She showed me her shotgun that had fallen apart again. The forearm was off. I told her, "After all the work I did so you could shoot a duck, you could have at least shot! You can shoot a shotgun without a forearm!" She looked at me and said, "No way, Dad! I watched 911 the other night, and a kid shot a broken shotgun and about killed himself!" What could I say? Girl hunters just think too much.

Smelt: Anyone who has never been up this way smelt fishing asks me, "What is a smelt?" How do I explain that a smelt is a little silver fish that is from around four to eight inches long? They run into the rivers and streams out of the Great Lakes in big schools to spawn. (There are also some found in inland lakes.) When the smelt runs peak, you will have hundreds and hundreds of people along the Great Lake streams trying to net them. Now, a smelt net is really a handnet. It is a little round net with usually a metal mesh v-shaped basket and a long handle. You dip the net into the schools of smelt and lift them out. It is nothing to fill a 5-gallon bucket with one dip when the smelt runs are in full swing.

A dip net is a net that runs off a pulley from a bridge or is operated off a long pole hanging out over the water. They can be up to nine foot square and are operated straight up and down for suckers and smelt. They are real popular in some areas downstate, but not so much so in the U.P.

People catch smelt by the truckloads, and then the fun begins. With smelt, you cook them and eat the bones and all. There is still the need to clean them, and this tends to take all the fun out of smelt fishing. It is nothing to sit five or six hours cleaning smelt steady. The way most people freeze them is to drop them down through the hole in a milk jug, then fill the jug full of water and freeze them in the water. You want to remember, they are best tasting when they are cooked fresh. In fact, when I take kids out smelting, I usually take a Coleman stove and cook them right on the beach. They are great then.

Mom's penalty: You have to remember that there is a down side to everything. The down side to living in an area like the U.P. with all the hunting and fishing is all the junk (all valuable) laying around the house all the time. Remember, sportsmen have to have a different item for each adventure they go off on. Now, Mom is the one who is expected to pick up all this stuff or know where it was placed nine or ten months ago when the fishermen last laid it down. All you women know good and well that a guy cannot be expected to remember where he puts everything to be sure and remember where it is now. I have stored items in a good safe place so I would be sure and find it when I wanted it and have never run across it to this day. But! I can remember picking it up and putting it in a secure place so I would be sure and be able to find it when I needed it again. That is why it is so important to stay on the good side of the lady of the house. You never know when you may need her.

Dear Friend,

I guess there is no way that I deserve all the blessings I have received in my life. God has been so good to me. I listened to my Dad while growing up and ended up with the job I always wanted since my high school days. While in the army I met and married my wife and God blessed us with four wonderful children. Now we have six grandchildren. I could go on and on talking about the blessings of God, but there is something more important I would like to tell you about. While in the army a friend gave me a book titled "The Greatest Story Ever Told". I read this book and it really got me thinking. Later I read the book called "What would Jesus do?" From these two books I started to wonder about Jesus dying on the cross once for all and I realized that all included me. After meeting my wife I asked the Lord to forgive my sins and come into my heart, but there was always a little question in my heart about being saved. A couple of years later I attended some special meetings being preached by a bear hunting friend of mine Evangelist Pete Rice. During these meetings I made sure about my salvation and have never had this doubt in my heart again.

Once I heard Brother Pete preach on John 3:16 "For God so loved the world that he gave his only begotten son, that whosoever believeth in Him should not perish, but have everlasting life". At the end of his preaching six people walked the isle to get saved. One was a tough, old, trapper that I knew and it really impressed me. What does being saved mean? It simply means that one understands that Jesus came and died on the cross for our sins, that we understand we are a sinner, and we ask Jesus to come into our heart, forgive our sins, and be our Savior.

You can use what is called the Romans Road to help you with this. It is as easy as driving down a 2-track out in the woods. If you would take a Bible you would find these verses. Romans 3:23 "All have sinned and come short of the glory of God." This means that all people have sinned and need to realize it. Romans 6:23 states, "the wages of sin is death". This means if we do not ask forgiveness of God for our sins we will die with payment due for them. I Corinthians 15:3 says, "Christ died for our sins". This means payment has already been paid in full for our sins by Jesus death on the cross. Romans 6:23 tells us, "the gift of God is eternal life through Jesus Christ our Lord". Everything that has to be done has been done, but for our part. Romans 10:13 tells us how, "Whosoever shall call upon the name of the Lord shall be saved". This means all a person has to do is understand they are a sinner, that Jesus died on the cross for them, and ask Him to come into their heart and forgive their sins. Then you like so many before you will have everlasting life to look forward to.

I pray you will do this and someday I will see you in heaven and you can tell me about it.

There are now six books available in the *Tales From A Game Warden* series.

Since retired Michigan Conservation Officer Sgt. John A. Walker published the first book there has been over 50,000 copies of his books self-published.

It has been a totally amazing project to see the way these books have been accepted by people in all walks of life. These family-style, humorous backwoods tales are all true just told in a way only a Yooper could tell them.

The six books and the order they were released are as follows:

1. A Deer Gets Revenge   ISBN 0-9639798-0-9

2. A Bucket of Bones   ISBN 0-9639798-1-7

3. Land of the Big Fish   ISBN 0-9639798-2-5

4. Luck, Skill, Stupidity   ISBN 0-9639798-3-3

5. Humans Are Nuts!   ISBN 0-9639798-4-1

6. But! But Honey it Wasn't My Fault
                    a.   ISBN 0-9639798-6-8

All these books can be ordered from JAW'S Publications, 530 Alger Ave. Manistique, MI 49854 or call 906-341-2082.

A single copy of any of these books cost $10.00 pp, but you get a special deal if you order a set of all six books for just $50.00 pp.